Simple Bicycle Repair

Simple Bicycle Repair

Fixing Your Bike Made Easy

Rob van der Plas

Cycle Publishing / Van der Plas Publications

Printed in Hong Kong

Publisher's information:
Cycle Publishing / Van der Plas Publications
1282 7th Avenue
San Francisco, CA 94122
USA
http://www.cyclepublishing.com
E-mail: pubrel@cyclepublishing.com

Distributed or represented to the book trade by:
USA: Midpoint Trade Books, Kansas City, KS
UK: Chris Lloyd Sales and Marketing Services/Orca Book
          Services, Poole, Dorset
Australia: Tower Books, Frenchs Forest, NSW

Cover design:
Kent Lytle, Lytle Design, Alameda, CA
Cover photograph by Belda Photography, Emeryville, CA

Photography for text:
Neil van der Plas, San Rafael, CA

With special thanks to *American Cyclery* in San Francisco
for providing equipment used for text and cover photos

Publisher's Cataloging in Publication Data
Van der Plas, Rob. Simple Bicycle Repair: Fixing Your Bike Made Easy.
1. Bicycles and bicycling — handbooks and manuals.
18.5 cm. p: 96. Includes index.
I. Title
II. Authorship
Library of Congress Control Number: 2003115533
ISBN 1-892495-43-0

Table of Contents

Contents

Introduction

About this Book

THE MODERN bicycle is a so-phisticated piece of equip-ment that's designed to last—provided it is maintained prop-erly and fixed as soon as some-thing does go wrong. That's the purpose of this book. In as few words, and in the clearest way possible, it shows how to take care of those things yourself. From a simple maintenance rou-tine to intricate gearing prob-lems, and from fixing a flat to suspension adjustments, it's all here, explained in a step-by-step format with clear color illustra-tions.

The first four chapters pro-vide all the information you need to carry out regular maintenance operations, while the individual maintenance and repair jobs are covered in the remaining chap-ters 5 through 17. In the back of the book, you'll find an extensive troubleshooting guide that will help you pinpoint the cause of any problem you may encoun-ter, as well as refer you to the section of the book where that operation is described in detail.

You and the Bike Shop

This book is not intended to compete with the services of a competent bicycle mechanic at a full-service bike shop. It covers the kind of things that the aver-age person can learn to carry out, whether by the roadside or in the home workshop.

However, some jobs are more difficult than that, and for those jobs (identified in the text), you should resort to a bike shop. The bike shop is also the place where you buy the parts and the tools which you may need when maintaining or repairing the bike.

CHAPTER 1

Know Your Bicycle

THERE ARE many different bicycle types on the market. However, whatever kind of bicycle you have, it will have most things in common with all other types. For purposes of repairing and maintaining it, you will want to look at it with the various functions of the parts of the machine in mind, and that's what this chapter will help you do.

Parts of the Bicycle

Fig. 1.1 shows the names for the most important parts of the bike. It will be easiest to understand them they are grouped together in functional groups, as follows:
• The Wheels
• The Drivetrain
• The Gearing System
• The Brakes
• The Steering System
• The Frameset
• Seat and Seatpost
• Suspension
• Accessories

The Wheels

One in front, the other in the rear, each wheel consists of a central hub, a bunch of spokes, and a rim on which the tire is installed. The wheels are probably the most frequent source of problems on the bike, and Chapters 5 through 7 are devoted to the various aspects of their maintenance and repair.

The Drivetrain

That's the name for the various components that transmit the rider's input to the rear wheel: pedals, cranks and chainrings (with the bearings, together called the crankset), chain, and freewheel with cogs on the rear wheel. Drivetrain work will be covered in Chapter 8.

The Gearing System

Most bikes are equipped with derailleur gearing, with derailleur mechanisms that shift the chain from one combination of chainring and cog to another to achieve a different gear ratio.

The other type relies on a mechanism built into the hub. Both types are controlled via flexible cables from levers that are usually installed on the handlebars. Maintenance of derailleur and hub gearing are covered in Chapters 9 and 10 respectively.

The Brakes

Here too, (usually) one in front and one on in the back. They come in different types, and most types are controlled via cables by means of levers on the

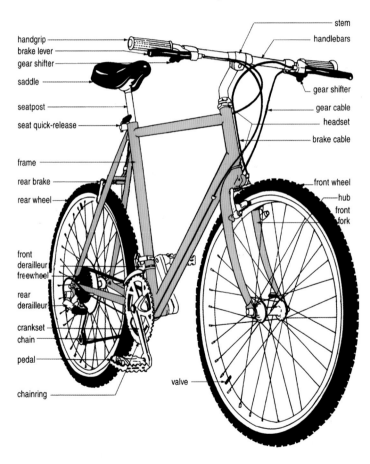

handgrip
brake lever
gear shifter
saddle
seatpost
seat quick-release
frame
rear brake
rear wheel
front derailleur
freewheel
rear derailleur
crankset
chain
pedal
chainring

stem
handlebars
gear shifter
gear cable
headset
brake cable
front wheel
hub
front fork
valve

Fig. 1.1. Parts of the bicycle.

handlebars. Their maintenance will be covered in Chapters 11 and 12 respectively.

The Steering System

The steering system comprises the handlebars, the front fork (in which the front wheel is held), and the ball bearing assembly called headset, which is installed in the frame's head tube. Chapter 13 is devoted to maintenance and repair jobs involving the steering system.

Seat and Seatpost

Although these items seem so simple, incorrect adjustment can be uncomfortable at least and dangerous in some cases. Chapter 14 shows you how to deal with these components.

The Frameset

That's the bike's backbone, to which all other parts are at-tached directly or indirectly. It consists of the frame itself and the front fork, which can also be regarded as part of the steering system. What litle maintenance is possible on frame and fork is covered in Chapter 15.

Suspension

Front suspension has become standard on many bikes, and rear suspension is not far behind. Chapter 16 is devoted to the various suspension adjustments and checks you can carry out yourself.

Accessories

You can attach lots of things to the bicycle, ranging from reflectors and lights to racks (luggage carriers), and from fenders (mudguards) to trip computers. Chapter 17 shows how to deal with the most common accessories.

CHAPTER 2

The Tools to Use

YOU WILL be able to handle most bicycle repair jobs with a very modest selection of tools. Yes, there are jobs that require more special tools, but none of these are so common that you should worry about them at this stage — that's what the bike shop is for. (Alternately, you can consider a more extensive repair text, such as my *Bicycle Repair Step by Step*.) This chapter describes the tools I recommend you buy right away, so you're prepared for anything that's likely to come your way as well as preventive maintenance.

Most of these tools can be purchased at almost any bike shop, although some of them are also available at general hardware stores. For that reason, I'll distinguish between "general tools," which are available at a hardware store, and "bicycle-specific tools" (marked with an asterisk in the descriptions below), which should only be bought at a bike shop.

When choosing your tools, make sure you get the highest quality available. Don't be fooled by terms like "economy tools," because in the long run, the only really economical tools are the good ones — not the cheap ones. If you see two similar looking tools at widely varying prices, get the more expensive one, because it's invariably the more accurate and more durable one. Cheap, inaccurate tools often don't last very long, but what's worse, nor will they be as comfortable to work with because they won't fit as accurately as they should. And what's worse, they may damage the parts of the bike, making it harder to carry out any work later on (even with good tools).

Tools to Carry

Here's a list of what I consider the absolute minimum in bicycle tools, which I recommend you carry on the bike, at least if the trip takes you beyond easy walking distance from your home. Refer to the accompanying illustrations (Figs. 2.1 and 2.2) for an idea as to what the individual tools look like.

2

1. Tire pump for the type of valve used on your bike ("Presta" valve or "Schrader" valve — see Chapter 6).*

2. Spare tube of a size that's compatible with the tires on your bike.*

3. Tire patch kit, containing patches, rubber solution, and sandpaper or scraper.*

4. Set of 3 tire levers (for a mountain bike, you only need 2).*

5. Set of Allen wrenches (also called Allen keys), at least in the sizes 4, 5, and 6 mm.

6. Needle-nose pliers.

7. Small regular and Phillips head screwdrivers.

8. Adjustable wrench ("Crescent wrench") in 6 in. or 8 in. length.

9. Crank tool (for older bikes, or a large Allen wrench for most modern bikes — see Chapter 8).*

10. Spoke wrench (nipple spanner), in the exact size for the spokes on your wheels.*

11. Small plastic bottle with thin-flowing lubricating oil.

Wrap it all up in a soft cloth, held all together with a strong rubber band or a strap. Items 5, 7, and 8 can often be purchased as one or more multi-purpose tools (mostly available only in bike shops). Except for the pump, all these items should fit in a small pouch that can be carried under the bike seat. Buy the bag after you've collected the tools, to make sure it's big enough.

Fig. 2.1. Collection of tools to carry on the bike.

Other Tools and Supplies

The tools listed above should be the core of your tool collection, and you'll find most jobs you ever encounter can be done without resorting to additional tools. However, for more exten-

---

* Items to buy at a bike shop

sive work on the bike at home, you may sooner or later decide to get some additional tools.

The only other items I suggest you buy at this point are a small tube of bearing grease, a bottle or spray-can of penetrating oil (to loosen stubborn screw-threaded items), and some cleaning and polishing materials — brushes in different sizes, a sponge, some more cleaning cloths, a bottle of bio-degradable bicycle polish, and a small can of wax (the kind sold in car part shops — *not* furniture wax). In addition, I recommend you get the following:

12. Full set of Allen wrenches (2 through 10 mm).

Fig. 2.2. Foreground: additional tools; background: workstand.

13. Pedal wrench.*

14. Set of combination wrenches (open-ended on one end, box-wrenches on the other end) in sizes 7 through 17.

15. Set of cone wrenches for work on the hubs.*

16. Chain tool, matched to the chain on your bike.*

17. Cable cutting tool.*

18. Cassette cog tool.*

Working on the Bike

For roadside repairs, most jobs can be carried out with the bike placed upside-down, resting on the handlebars and the seat. With most modern bikes, that's OK, as long as you remove any items mounted on the handle-bars. On older road bikes, support the handlebars so that the cables don't get kinked.

When working on the bike at home, it'll be nicest if you can invest in a special work stand, such as the ones made by Park and Blackburn. A low-budget alternative is to hang the bike with home-made hooks and ropes from two big eye-bolts attached to the ceiling.

Basic Maintenance Procedures

THERE ARE a number of items common enough in several locations on (almost) any bike to justify specific handling instructions. This will obviate the need for repeated instructions for all the parts where they occur. They are the following:

• Screw-Threaded Connections
• Quick-Releases
• Cable Controls
• Ball Bearings

These are the items covered in this chapter. If you need specific instructions in conjunction with any of the procedures described elsewhere in the book, this chapter will be the place to refer to.

Screw-Threaded Connections

Most bicycle parts are attached, held in place, or assembled by means of screw-threads. In some cases that's obvious enough, when talking about nuts and bolts, but it also applies to the less obvious ones, such as the parts of ball bearings and the assembly of gear or brake mechanisms.

All screw-threaded connections comprise a cylindrical part with a helical groove cut around the circumference (the male part, which may be a bolt or an axle) and a hollow part with a matching groove cut around the inside of the circular hole (the female part, which may be a nut).

Usually, turning clockwise tightens the connection, and that's referred to as right-hand thread. A few parts have left-hand thread. which is tightened by turning clockwise, loosened by turning counterclockwise.

There should be a washer (a

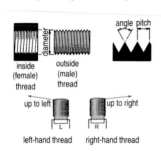

Fig. 3.1 Screw-thread details.

flat metal ring) between the fe-male part and any other part that is clamped or screwed in under-neath. This reduces the friction, making it easier to tighten and loosen the connection. Some-times the washer is "keyed," which means it can only be in-serted in a specific orientation (especially between screwed parts of adjustable ball bearings) to allow tightening the one part without affecting the adjustment of the other part.

Screw-threads are identified by the outside diameter of the male part, usually measured in mm (millimeters). Even though the diameter of two threaded connections may be the same, there are other aspects in which they can differ.

When replacing bolts and nuts, be careful to use only met-ric ones. In some sizes, it is hard to tell metric and "Standard" (or Whitworth) nuts and bolts apart. Mixing them would ruin the components due to the differ-ence in thread pattern.

To tighten or loosen a screwed connection, one part has to be turned in the appropri-ate direction with a precisely fit-ting tool with enough leverage, while the other part must be held steady. In the case of a nut-and-bolt connection, hold each part with a wrench; in the case of

something screwed directly into the bicycle frame, hold the frame by hand or under the force of a work stand.

If you have difficulty loosen-ing a connection that's been in place for a long time, spray some penetrating oil at the point where the male part engages the female, and wait 2–3 minutes before trying again.

When reinstalling screwed connections, make sure they are clean, undamaged, and not cor-roded; and if needed, clean, lu-bricate, and/or replace them with new parts. Always use a smooth washer under the head of any nut to reduce friction.

Bolts come in a variety of head shapes. The Allen head has become quite prevalent on

Fig. 3.2. Use of two wrenches to tighten or loosen a screwed connection.

3

bicycle components. It has a hexagonal recess, and the matching tool does less damage than other tools do to regular screw cuts and hexagonal bolt heads.

To prevent accidental loosening of screwed connections, there are a number of different solutions. Sometimes, a double set of nuts is used, a thin so-called locknut and a regular nut, which are tightened against each other for a more effective hold.

Accessories should always be held with a minimum of two screws or bolts in order to minimize the effect of the unsupported mass that would cause parts to vibrate loose if held in only one spot.

When tightening or loosening threaded connections, do

Fig. 3.3. Screw thread is used on many parts besides nuts and bolts, like on this bottom bracket.

not apply more torque than required — to avoid damaging the head of the bolt or some other part. For this reason, choose tools of a length that's commensurate with the part in question. A 5 mm bolt or nut should not be handled with a 10-inch long adjustable wrench but with a 5 mm fixed wrench, which will have an appropriate length, resulting in the correct torque.

Especially large aluminum screw-threaded components should be handled with great care to avoid damage to the screw thread. Use only the specific tools made for these components.

When screw-threaded connections are used for adjustment, there will be one male and two female components. The latter two are tightened against each other once the correct adjustment has been established. Since this is most commonly done on adjustable ball bearings on the bike, this will be described under *Ball Bearings* elsewhere in this chapter.

Quick-Releases

These devices are most frequently used on the wheels to allow easy removal and installation of the wheels. The same principle of operation is also found on many brakes, in order to open them up far enough for easy wheel removal, and on the clamp that holds the seat to facilitate easy seat height adjustment. They all work on the same principle, which involves a cam-shaped device connected to a lever that can be partially rotated to tighten or loosen a connection. In most cases, the cam is hidden inside some other part, so it's hard to figure out how it works without a drawing.

When the lever is in the "open" position, the small end of the cam is engaged, leaving the connection loose. When the lever is placed in the "closed" position, the long end of the cam is pushed just past the engagement, which ensures that the tension is high enough, while preventing accidental loosening.

If the lever is not marked with the words "open" and "close," you can still tell which is which by observing what happens when you move the lever from one position to the other. Most modern levers are shaped with a convex (bulged) surface that faces out when closed and a concave (cupped) surfaces showing when open.

Once the adjustment is correct, operate only the lever, *not* the thumbnut, which should be

left alone whenever possible. Unfortunately, the custom of equipping the tips of front forks of bicycles with ridges (to prevent accidental wheel release) makes it impossible to use the quick-release mechanism of the hub the way it was intended.

You can still loosen and tighten the mechanism properly just using the lever, but the ridges on the ends of the fork blades require you to loosen the thumb nut to provide enough clearance to slip over these ridges when removing or installing the wheel. When reinstalling the wheel, you'll have to screw it back on once the wheel is in place for the quick-release lever to become functional again. Here's how you handle a quick-release connection.

Quick-release procedure:

1. Set the lever in the "open"

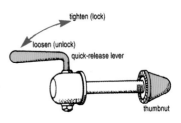

Fig. 3.4. Principle of quick-release mechanism.

position.

2. Place the device (wheel, brake, seatpost) in position. If it can't be done, loosen the thumb nut until things fit.

3. Place the device in the desired position and orientation.

4. Screw in the thumb nut until all slack is taken up, but don't forcibly tighten it.

5. Flip the lever over into the "closed" position, if possible — if it cannot be moved fully into the "closed" position, unscrew the locknut in half-turn increments until it the lever can be closed with firm hand force.

6. Check once more whether

Fig. 3.5. Closing the quick-release lever on a wheel hub.

the device is aligned properly and if not, loosen, then retighten it in the correct position.

Cable Controls

Flexible cable controls are commonly used on the bicycle to operate hand brakes and gear shifting devices. They're also known by the name "Bowden cables."

Each cable combines a flexible stranded inner cable, or wire, with a flexible but incompressible hollow cover, or sleeve. The inner cable takes up tension (i.e. pulling) forces, whereas the cover takes up compression (pushing) forces. The ends of the cover are held in fixed cup-shaped attachments, while the inner wire has a soldered- or crimped-on nipple at one end and is clamped in at the other end.

Many gear cables are sold only as matched sets with dimensions that are specific to a particular make and model. Otherwise, you can just buy cover by the foot or the meter and the inner cable in sections long enough to match any application (just make sure the nipple has the right shape and the cable has the same diameter as the original cable used, so it's of similar strength and flexibility), and cut to length once installed.

To prevent corrosion and keep them moving freely, apply some lubricant between the inner cable and the outer sleeve.

The tension of any control cable is adjusted by means of a barrel adjuster, which works in conjunction with the clamping attachment for the inner cable. Although you can usually adjust the system adequately just using this device, you may at times have to undo the clamping nut or screw and clamp the cable in at a different point.

Cable adjusting procedure:

1. Check to make sure any quick-release device that may be provided in the system is tensioned, and if not, tension it.

2. Verify whether it's still "out of adjustment" once the quick-release is set properly. If not, proceed to Step 3.

3. Loosen the locknut by several turns.

4. Turn the adjusting barrel out relative to the part into which it is screwed (to increase) or in (to reduce) the tension on the cable. Loosening will open up the brake or make

the derailleur shift later; tightening will do the opposite.

5. Holding the adjusting barrel with one hand, tighten the locknut again.

6. Check to make sure the mechanism is adjusted as intended and if not, repeat until it is.

Note:

On many newer road bikes, there is an adjuster without a locknut installed on one of the brake levers or on the derailleur. In that case, instead of following Steps 3 through 5, merely turn the adjuster out or in to achieve tightening or loosening, respectively. In case of the brakes, this only works properly if you first undo the brake quick-release — and tension it again afterwards.

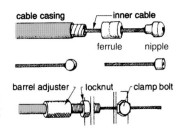

Fig. 3.6. Cable and cable adjuster details.

If the adjustment cannot be achieved this way, the end of the cable must be clamped in at a different point — further in to tighten, out to loosen the cable.

Cable clamping procedure:

1. First release tension on the cable — either using the quick-release device, if provided, or at the barrel adjuster per Steps 3 and 4 of the *Cable adjusting procedure*.

2. Loosen the clamp nut or bolt that holds the end of the cable, using a fitting tool.

3. Using e.g., needle-nose pliers, pull the cable into the appropriate position — usually no more than ¼ inch (6 mm) from its original clamping position.

4. While holding the cable in place with the pliers, tighten the clamp bolt firmly.

5. Carry out an adjustment per the above *Cable adjusting procedure*.

Ball Bearings

Two different types of ball bearings are in use on the bike: adjustable and non-adjustable ones. The latter are referred to as sealed bearings, machine bearings, or cartridge bearings.

A cup-and-cone bearing consists of a cup-shaped bearing race and a cone-shaped one, between which the bearing balls are contained, embedded in lubricant. One of the two parts (cone or cup) is adjustable by means of a screw-threaded connection, and is locked in position once it is properly adjusted by means of a lockring screwed up tightly and an intermediate keyed washer (stopped against rotation by means of a lip or flat section that engages a corresponding section of the male part).

The advantage of the cup-and-cone bearing is that it can be adjusted to compensate for wear. To do that, the cup and

Fig. 3.7. Cable clamping detail.

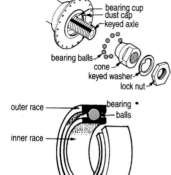

Fig. 3.8. Top: cup-and-cone bearing. Bottom: cartridge bearing.

the cone are screwed closer together, reducing the space for the bearing balls slightly, tightening the bearing.

The cartridge bearing consists of pre-assembled non-adjustable components. When these bearings get worn or damaged, the entire bearing assembly, or "cartridge," has to be pulled off and replaced, requiring a special matching tool, all of which should be left to a bike mechanic.

Bearing adjusting procedure:

1. Loosen the locknut at the end of the bearing assembly, holding the underlying part firmly with a matching tool.

2. Lift the keyed washer clear off the cone, e.g. with a small screw driver.

3. Turn the screwed component (usually the cone) in (to tighten) or out (to loosen).

4. Tighten the locknut again, while holding the cone or the bearing race with another tool.

When you tighten the two screw-threaded parts against each other, the bearing will be tightened a little more; so first adjust it loosely, before you tighten the locknut. Even so, check to make sure the bearing is adjusted to run smoothly without noticeable play — and if not, tighten or loosen the parts a little, and repeat the operation until they do.

Lubrication is usually done with bearing grease. Before lubricating a bearing, though, it must be thoroughly cleaned out with solvent and a clean cloth. Never spray thin spray lubricant at ball bearings in an effort to lubricate them: that is more likely to introduce surface dirt into the bearing and wash out any lubricant inside than it is to act as an effective way of lubricating the bearing.

Preventive Maintenance

PREVENTIVE maintenance minimizes the risk of mishaps while riding the bike. This chapter presents a schedule of regular checks to keep your bike going reliably. These jobs are categorized as pre-ride, monthly, and annual inspections.

Fig. 4.1. Testing the front brake operation.

Pre-Ride Inspection

The reason I suggest you check these items each day you take out the bike is so they become routine. It only takes a few minutes.

Procedure:

1. Check the quick-releases on the wheels and on the brakes to make sure they're in the closed position. Loosen them first, and then retighten them. They should require firm force to tighten. Refer to Chapter 3.

2. Check the brakes, which should block rotation of the wheels when the levers are pulled to within ¾ inch (2 cm) from the handlebars. Apply each lever in turn while pushing down and forward on the bike. If required, adjust per Chapter 11 or 12.

3. Check to make sure the handlebars are straight and firm. To do that, straddle the front wheel, holding it tightly between your legs, and apply force to the handlebars, while trying to twist them in the horizontal and vertical

plane. If needed, adjust and tighten per Chapter 13.

4. Especially if others sometimes ride your bike too, check to make sure the seat is at the right height for you, straight, and firmly clamped in. Adjust and tighten per Chapter 14 if not.

5. Check whether the tires are inflated properly. Inflate if necessary.

6. Check operation of the gears by lifting the rear wheel off the ground and trying to engage each gear combination while turning the pedals. If needed, adjust per Chapter 9 or 10.

7. Spin each wheel, while lifted off the ground, to check whether they turn smoothly, without interference or visible wobbling. Straighten per Chapter 7 if necessary.

Monthly Inspection

This inspection consists of a more thorough check and some routine maintenance operations to make up for wear, but also includes cleaning and lubrication.

Be alert to any signs of damage in addition to those specifically mentioned here. Fix or replace such items as soon as you notice them. Ask for advice at a bike shop if you're not sure whether something is serious enough to warrant replacement.

Procedure:

1. Cleaning

Clean the bike and apply protective coating as described under *Cleaning the Bike.*

2. Lubrication

Lubricate the following parts:

- The chain, spraying on a special chain spray lubricant

Fig. 4.2.
Lubrication points
for monthly
inspection.

available at a bike shop.

- Brake levers, shifters, pivot points of exposed mechanisms, and cable ends, using thin spray lubricant, aiming carefully with the thin tubular nozzle extension.

- Afterwards, wipe off all excess lubricants to prevent parts of your bike becoming sticky and attracting dirt.

3. General check

Follow all the Steps described under Pre-Ride Inspection.

4. Wheel bearings

Check the wheels for loose bearings (applying sideways force at the rim while holding the front fork for the front wheel, or the frame for the rear wheel). If the wheel moves sideways, the bearings have to be adjusted as per Chapters 3 and 7.

5. Wheel rim and spokes

Check the wheels for wobble and loose, bent, or broken spokes. Wheel wobble is checked by lifting the wheel off the ground and looking at it from behind at a fixed point while rotating it. Refer problems to a bike shop or see Chapter 7.

6. Tires and tubes

Check the tires for damage and significant wear. Replace them if there are bulges, cuts, or seriously worn areas. Remove any embedded objects and replace the tube if it has been losing pressure from one day to the next. See Chapter 6.

7. Brakes

Check the operation of the brakes and, if the bike has rim brakes, observe whether the brake pads touch the rim squarely over their entire length and width when you pull the brake lever to within about ¾ inch (2 cm) from the handlebars. Adjust if necessary, referring to Chapter 11 or 12.

8. Cranks

Using either the wrench part of the crank tool or a fitting Allen wrench (depending on the crank attachment detail), tighten the bolts that hold the cranks to the bottom bracket spindle. You may have to remove a dust cap first (and reinstall it afterward). See Chapter 8.

9. Suspension

Wipe any dirt off the suspension components, wiping away from the seals. Then make sure any rear suspension pivot bolts are firmly held, and apply a drop of lubricant to each pivot point.

10. Accessories

Inspect any accessories installed on the bike, as well as any you keep at home for occasional use. Make sure they are functional, and fix them if not. Tighten the mounting hardware for anything installed on the bike.

11. Final check

Carefully go over the entire bike and check to make sure all nuts and bolts are in place and tightened, nothing is loose, and no parts are missing or damaged.

Annual Inspection

This is essentially a complete overhaul, to be carried out after a year's intensive use. If you ride in really bad weather and muddy terrain a lot, you should carry out this inspection twice a year.

Get any overhauling or replacement work carried out by the bike shop. But before you do, thoroughly clean the bike and go over it as described for the monthly inspection. This will minimize the amount of work the bike shop has to do, saving you some money.

Cleaning the Bike

Although it's recommended to clean your bike once a month, it may have to be done more frequently if you ride in wet and dirty terrain a lot — in fact, after every such ride. Depending on the weather and the terrain, the nature of the dirt can be quite different.

In wet weather, it's important to avoid corrosion and thus necessary to use wax and lubricants rather generously. However, when it's dry and dusty, open lubricated parts are actually a hazard because of their tendency to hold fine dry dust particles that

Fig. 4.3. Cleaning in hard-to-reach places on the bike.

work like an abrasive, causing wear and rough operation of moving parts and controls.

Keep this in mind, while otherwise generally following the following procedure.

Procedure:

1. If the bike is dry, wipe it clean as much as possible with a soft brush or a clean cloth to remove any loose dust. If the bike is wet or the dirt is caked on, clean the bike with a bucket full of water and a sponge. Don't use a hose with a strong spray nozzle, to avoid getting water into the bearings and other sensitive parts. After washing the frame itself, take each of the other components and thoroughly clean around them.

2. Use a clean, dry cloth to dry off all the parts that got wet in the preceding operation.

3. Use a solvent-soaked cloth to clean the tight corners of the bike and its components and accessories — from the areas around the spokes to those behind the brakes and the nooks and crannies of the derailleurs. Many of the smallest corners are best reached by wrapping the cloth around a thin, narrow object, such as a screwdriver.

4. To protect the areas you've just cleaned under Step 3, do the same with a cloth soaked in lubricant or wax (use wax for dry weather, oil if it's more likely to be wet).
   • You can combine Steps 3 and 4 by soaking the cloth in a mixture of solvent with about 10 percent mineral oil.

5. Treat all metal surfaces of the bike and its parts with wax. If the paint or the metal surfaces appear to be weathered, you can use an automotive liquid wax.

6. Rub out the wax coating with a clean, dry, soft cloth.

7. Treat all non-metallic surfaces, such as plastic with Armor-All or a similar material for treating plastic parts of cars. Spray it onto a clean cloth, and rub it out.

CHAPTER 5

Wheel Removal & Installation

MOST WHEEL and tire problems — dealt with in the next two chapters — require the wheel to be removed from the bicycle. What's involved depends on the following factors:

• Front or rear wheel

• Held in with quick-release or axle nuts

• Regular wheel or one with e.g., a disk or hub brake or hub gearing.

Here are general procedures, distinguishing between front and rear wheels, with notes to cover the other special cases.

Replace Front Wheel

Removal procedure:

1. Open up the brake's quick-release or cable attachment to spread the brake arms apart so the tire can pass between the brake pads (if the bike has rim brakes).

   If there is no easy way to release the brake, you can either let the air out of the tire or undo the brake cable connection. If it is a wheel with another type of brake, such as a drum or disk brake, undo the attachment of the brake control and dislodge the counter lever — see the instructions in Chapter 12. In the rare instance of a wheel with an electric generator, or dynamo, built in, disconnect the electric wires.

Fig. 5.1. Releasing V-brake cable to remove or install wheel.

2. Twist the hub quick-release lever into the "open" position, or undo the hub axle nuts on both sides.

3. If the front fork has ridges or some other component to stop the wheel, unscrew the quick-release's thumbnut until the hub can be removed.

4. Slide the wheel out, guiding it at the hub and the rim.

Installation procedure:

1. If necessary, follow the same procedure as described in Step 1 above for wheel removal, so the wheel will pass between the brake pads.

2. Make sure the hub's quick-release lever is in the "open"

Fig. 5.2. Releasing side-pull brake.

position or the axle nuts are unscrewed far enough (with the washers pushed to the outside).

3. If there are ridges on the fork ends, unscrew the quick-release's thumbnut, or the axle nuts, far enough for the wheel to clear them.

4. Slide the wheel over the fork ends, guiding it near the rim between the brake pads (if the bike has rim brakes) until the hub is seated fully at the end of the slots in the fork ends.

5. Center the wheel at the rim between the fork blades (leaving the same distance on both sides) and tighten the quick-release lever or the axle nuts. (If there are ridges on the fork tips, first screw in the thumbnut until the lever can be tightened fully with significant hand force).

6. Redo any attachments and adjustments that were affected by the removal of the wheel (see Step 1 of the preceding *Removal procedure*).

Replace Rear Wheel

Removal procedure:

1. If it's a bike with derailleur gearing, select the gear that engages the smallest cog in the back and the smallest chainring in the front.

2. Open up the brake's quick-release or cable attachment to spread the brake arms apart, so the tire can pass between the brake pads (if the bike has rim brakes).
   • If there is no quick-release on the brake, you can either let the air out of the tire or undo the brake cable connection.
   • If it is a wheel with a disk brake or a hub brake, undo the attachment of the control cable at the brake and dislodge the counter lever — see the instructions in Chapter 9. In case it's a wheel with a hub gear, select the highest gear and then disconnect the control for the hub gear — see Chapter 12.

3. For derailleur gearing, hold back the derailleur with the chain as shown in Fig. 5.3 to provide a straight path, unobstructed by the routing of the chain around the derailleur pulleys.

4. Twist the hub quick-release lever into the "open" posi-

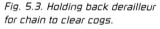

Fig. 5.3. Holding back derailleur for chain to clear cogs.

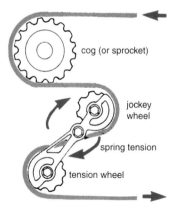

cog (or sprocket)

jockey wheel

spring tension

tension wheel

Fig. 5.4. Chain routing at rear derailleur.

Fig. 5.5. Tightening or loosening axle nut.

tion, or undo the axle nuts.

5. Slide the wheel out, guiding it by the hub and at the rim.

Installation procedure:

1. If applicable, follow the instructions in Step 1 of the Wheel removal procedure, so the wheel will pass between the brake pads.

2. Make sure the hub's quick-release lever is set to the "open" position, or the axle nuts are screwed out, with the washers snug against them.

4. Slide the wheel into the slot in the dropouts, guiding it near the rim between the brake pads (if the bike has rim brakes).

5. On a derailleur-geared bike, make sure the chain engages the smallest chainring in the front and the rear derailleur is set for the gear in which the chain engages the smallest cog, and route the chain over that smallest cog and around the pulleys as shown in Fig. 5.4.

6. Center the wheel at the rim between the seat stays (leaving the same distance on both sides) and tighten the quick-release lever. (If it can't be tightened fully or if it is too loose, adjust the thumbnut until the lever can be tightened fully with significant hand force). If it's a wheel with axle nuts, tighten them firmly and equally.

6. Redo any attachments and adjustments that were affected by the removal of the wheel (see Step 1 of the *Removal procedure*).

CHAPTER 6

Tire & Tube Maintenance

ON ALMOST all bikes, each tire comprises a separate (inner) tube and an (outer) tire cover. The cover sits around the tube and is held onto the rim by means of metal wires, or "beads" that are embedded in the sidewalls.

The tube has a valve to control the air pressure, and two different valve types are in use — Presta or Schrader. Make sure you get tubes with the same type of valves as the existing ones on your bike. Also make sure the pump matches the valve.

Tire covers are designated by their nominal size, like "26 x 1.75" for a typical mountain bike tire, meaning the tire's outside diameter is approximately 26 in. and its width about 1¾ in. When replacing the tire cover, make sure you get (approximately) the same size as was on the bike, and when replacing a tube, make sure it suits that tire size.

Tire Inflation

Inflate the tire whenever the pressure is inadequate. It should have at least the pressure marked on the sidewall. Ideally, use a pump with a pressure gauge — or a separate gauge.

Procedure:

1. Make sure to use the right pump and a pressure gauge for the type of valve on the tire.

2. Check whether the valve is straight in the rim (if it isn't, let all the air out, straighten it out by manipulating the tire sidewall all around, pushing the tire with the tube in the appropriate direction).

Fig. 6.1. Inflating a tire.

3. Remove the dust cap that may be screwed on the end of the valve.

4 Depending on the type of valve:
   • If you're dealing with a Presta valve, unscrew the little round nut at the end and briefly push in the pin in the end to which the nut is attached to loosen it.
   • If the bike has a Schrader valve, briefly push in the internal pin to loosen it. Try not to let too much air escape.

5. Place the pump head square onto the valve, avoiding the escape of air; make sure it is seated properly on the valve and, if the pump has a toggle lever, flip it to clamp the valve head around the valve.

6. Holding the pump under a right angle to the valve, inflate the tire to the desired pressure.

7. If the valve is of the Presta type, tighten the nut at the end; reinstall the dust cap.

Tube Replacement

The easiest and quickest way to "fix" a bike with a punctured tire is to replace the inner tube. Before commencing, remove the wheel from the bike, following the instructions in Chapter 5.

Procedure:

1. Remove the dust cap from the valve and let any remaining air out of the tire by pushing in the pin in the valve (after unscrewing the

Fig. 6.2. Inserting tire lever.

Fig. 6.3. Removing the tire.

little round nut in the case of a Presta valve).

2. If there is a nut screwed onto the base of the valve, remove it.

3. Push the valve into the tire as far as possible to create more space for the tire bead toward the center of the rim.

4. Manipulate the tire sidewall by hand, working all around to push the bead toward the deeper center section of the rim, then work one area of the side from which you're working, some distance away from the valve, back up to the edge of the rim.

5. Place the end of the long part of the L-shaped tire lever under the tire bead, over the side of the rim, with the short end of the tire lever facing toward the center of the wheel. Then leverage it to push the bead of the tire up and over the side of the rim, hooking the notched end of the lever around a spoke.

6. Do the same with the second tire lever, about 4 spokes further to one side.

7. If necessary, do the same with the third tire lever on the other side.

8. Use either a tire lever or your fingers, push the sidewall off the rim all around.

9. Pull most of the inner tube out.

10. Push the valve through the valve hole and remove the tube.

11. Check the condition of the tire cover inside and out, and remove any sharp embedded objects (using tweezers if necessary).

12. Check the condition of the rim tape that covers the deepest section of the rim bed to make sure it is intact and no spoke ends are poking through (replace the rim tape and/or file off protruding spoke ends, if necessary).

Fig. 6.4. Reseating tire sidewall.

13. Install the new tube starting at the valve, carefully making sure it is embedded properly in the deepest section of the rim under the tire.

14. Inflate the tube just a little so it is no longer "limp" but does not have noticeable pressure either.

15. Starting at the valve, pull the tire cover back over the rim, working it into the deepest section of the rim as you work your way around in both directions until it is in place over its entire circumference. The last part will probably be tough, but don't use a tire lever or any other tool to do this — instead, achieve enough slack by working the bead deeper into the center section and pulling the entire tire toward the valve (you may have to let more air out of the tube), then pull the last section over from the opposite side as shown in Fig. 6.4

16. Inflate the tube slightly and then "knead" the sidewalls until you're sure no part of the inner tube is pinched between the rim and the tire bead.

17. Inflate the tube to its final pressure, making sure tube and cover are seated properly as you do so. The ridge on the sidewall must be the same distance from the rim all around the circumference on both sides. If necessary, correct it by first letting some air out, then working all around the tire until it is seated properly, and then re-inflating the tire.

18. Check the pressure and correct it, if necessary.

Patching the Tube

If you don't have (any more) spare tires with you, or once you get home, you can usually repair a damaged tube by patching it. Most of the work is the same as what was described above for replacing the tube, so this description only covers the actual patching. To get to that stage when you have to do this by the roadside, or whenever you have to repair the tube that's installed on the bike, first carry out Steps 1 through 11 of the procedure *Tube Replacement*. And when you are done patching the inner tube, resume work at Step 12 of that procedure.

Tools and equipment:

• tire patch kit (adhesive

patches, sand paper or abrasive scraper, rubber solution, and talcum powder)

Procedure:

1. Check the entire surface of the tube, starting at any location you may have identified as the probable cause of the puncture on account of damage to the tire.

2. If you can't easily find the location of the leak, inflate the tube and pass it along your ear or your eye, to listen or feel where air escapes. If you don't find it this way, dip the inflated tube in a basin with water and watch for escaping air bubbles — that's the location of the hole (but continue checking, since there may be more than one). If you have dipped the tire, dry it before proceeding. Mark the location of the leak(s) by drawing a circle that's bigger than the patch you will be using.

3. Rough up the area with the abrasive from the tire patch kit and wipe it clean.

4. Apply a thin, even layer of rubber solution to the area to be patched, slightly bigger than the patch you have selected, and let it dry for

about 1 minute in hot weather, 2–3 minutes in cold weather.

5. Pull one end of the protective layer (usually aluminum foil) from the patch, without touching the adhesive side, and apply it to the treated area of the tube, with the hole in the center, while pulling off the remainder of the protective layer.

6. Apply firm pressure to the entire patch for about a minute, squeezing it by hand and rubbing it, e.g., with the handle of a screwdriver while supporting the tire.

7. Check to make sure the patch has adhered properly over its entire surface (and

Fig. 6.5. Applying rubber solution to patch area.

Fig. 6.6. Applying the patch.

redo Steps 3 through 6 if it
has not).

8. Sprinkle some talcum powder over the patched area to
   prevent it from adhering to
   the inside of the tire cover.
   (Leaving the transparent
   plastic on the non-adhesive
   side of the patch has the
   same effect.)

9. Inflate the tube and wait
   about a minute to make sure
   it is not leaking, and if it is,
   repeat the repair for the
   same or any other hole you
   find.

10. Let the air out again and re-
    install the tube under the tire
    cover over the rim as out-
    lined in Steps 12 through 18

of the procedure *Tube Replacement.*

Note:

Make sure the rim tape is installed properly in the middle of
the rim, covering the spoke nipples, and replace it if it is damaged or missing.

Replace or Repair the Tire Cover

Occasionally, you may be able
to patch a tire cover if it has a
small cut in it. However, it will be
better to replace the tire completely if you can. If you do
choose to patch it, follow the instructions above for tube repair
and patch the inside of the cover
with a small section cut from an
old, thin tire. Use rubber adhesive on both the inside of the tire
and on the patch. Sprinkle some
talcum powder over the patch to
prevent adhesion of the tube to
the tire cover.

    To replace the cover, follow
the procedure *Tube Replacement* but remove the tire cover.
Then install the new cover on
one side, reinsert the tube, and
follow the rest of the description.

CHAPTER 7

Wheel Maintenance

BESIDES flat tires, the other wheel problems are broken spokes, bent rims, and bad hub bearings. To understand these issues, note how a wheel is built up of hub, spokes, and rim. It's the spoke tension that keeps the wheel together.

Wheel Problems

Wheel damage usually originates with a blow to the rim, deforming it either radially or laterally. When it is deformed this way, it's called "out of true," and the trick is to get it "trued" again. Some of the spokes become looser and others tighter, and some may be broken. First check the extent of the damage as follows.

Inspection procedure:

1. Place the bike upside down (protecting any items mounted on the handlebars, if necessary).

2. Slowly spin the wheel, checking the distance between each side of the rim and the frame. Observe whether the wheel wobbles sideways, in which case it's laterally out of true, or radially (the outside of the wheel seems to wobble up-and-down as it rotates). Also check whether any of the spokes are broken.

3. If there appears to be a gradual deformation over a significant area, you will probably be able to fix it, following the description *Wheel Truing*.

4. If there is a short, sudden deformation, it is probably due to direct-impact damage of

Fig. 7.1. Checking wheel truing with the wheel on the bike.

the rim, which cannot be re-paired satisfactorily, and should be solved by having a bike shop replace the rim.

Wheel Truing

This is the work necessary to get the wheel back into shape if your wheel truing check has estab-lished that it wobbles either side-ways (i.e., it is laterally out of true) or up-and-down (i.e., it is radially out of true).

Lateral truing procedure:

1. On the basis of the wheel truing check described above, mark which section of the wheel is too far to the left or the right relative to the center between the two sides

Fig. 7.2. Use of spoke wrench when truing a wheel.

of the seat stays or the front fork blades.

2. In the area thus marked, loosen the spokes that lead to the same side as to which the buckle deviates from the center, and tighten the spokes that run to the other side. Do this by turning the nipples with the spoke wrench — about one turn at the highest point of the buckle and gradually less to ¼ turn to the ones near the end of the buckled portion.
   • Looking from the center of the wheel toward the rim, loos-ening is when you turn clock-wise, and tightening when you turn counterclockwise.

3. Repeat Step 2 (but turning the nipples less and less as you get closer to the desired effect) until the sideways wobble is eliminated.

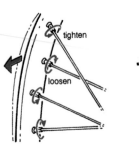

Fig. 7.3. Lateral wheel truing.

Radial truing procedure:

Using the same techniques as described in Step 1 of the preceding *Lateral truing procedure*, identify the "flat spot" or the "high spot" of the rim by marking the nearest spokes. Then loosen the spokes in the "flat" area and tighten the ones in the "high" area until the up-and-down wobble, or "hop," is eliminated (i.e., the wheel is radially true), proceeding as in Steps 2 and 3 of the preceding *Lateral truing procedure*.

Emergency Buckled Wheel Repair

If the damage occurs suddenly during a ride in the form of a badly buckled wheel, e.g., as a result of hitting an obstacle, you may be able to make a provi-

sional repair by the roadside. Ride very carefully after this, and once you get home, let the bike shop rebuild the wheel.

Procedure:

1. Remove the wheel from the bike.

2. Find a suitable step, such as a curb stone, on which you can support one part of the rim while the other part is supported at a lower point and the hub axle stays clear of the road surface. Place the wheel so that the most severe part of the outward deformation faces down on the higher support point.

Fig. 7.5. Emergency repair of a buckled wheel.

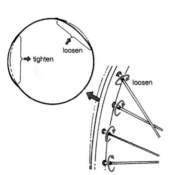

Fig. 7.4. Radial wheel truing.

3. Push down on the sections of the rim that are 90 degrees offset either side of the buckled portion. Continue or repeat until the rim is reasonably straight.

4. Place the wheel back in the bike and do a truing check as described above, then adjust the spoke tension as well as possible under the circumstances until the wobble is minimized.

Replacing Spokes

When a spoke breaks, you want to replace it as soon as possible. They come in a large number of sizes (with matching nipples), depending on the size and model of rim, hub, and spoking pattern. Get the bike shop to recommend the right size to use as spares, and carry some on long trips.

Procedure:

1. Remove the remaining piece (or pieces) of the broken spoke, unscrewing the outside portion from the nipple.

2. Buy a spoke that's exactly the same length and thickness as the other spokes on the same side of the wheel.
   • If the spoke is very loose in the nipple, also replace the nipple: remove a section of the tire and the tube as described in Chapter 6, lifting the rim tape, and pry out the old nipple. Then insert the new one and reinstall the rim tape, the tube, and the tire.

Fig. 7.7. Replacing a broken spoke.

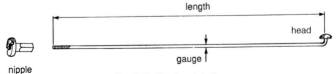

length

head

gauge

nipple

Fig. 7.6. Spoke details.

3. Route the new spoke the same way as the one in the second hub flange hole from the spoke to be replaced run — with the head on the inside or the outside, and passing over or under the various crossing spokes.

4. Apply a little lubricant to the threaded end of the spoke and then route the new spoke the same way as the one you observed in Step 3, screwing the nipple onto the end of the spoke until it has the same tension as other spokes on the same side of the wheel.

5. Check the wheel and make any truing corrections that may be necessary, following the description *Wheel Truing* starting on page 37.

The Hubs

The hub consists of an axle, a set of ball bearings, and the hub body. On the sides, the hub body has flanges to accommodate the holes through which the spokes are inserted. Quick-release hubs have hollow axles, while they are solid for "bolted-on" hubs, i.e., those held on with axle nuts.

The ball bearings may be either adjustable cup-and-cone bearings or cartridge bearings. Hub maintenance consists of adjusting, lubricating, and overhauling.

All this work can be done with the wheel left assembled. If the wheel either runs rough or it is loose (during the monthly inspection or if you suspect a problem), the bearings should be adjusted. That's only possible on cup-and-cone bearing hubs, so check with the bike shop what kind you have.

Hub Bearing Adjustment

To do this, you'll need a pair of cone wrenches, in addition to the roadside tools recom-

Fig. 7.8. Adjusting hub bearings (cup-and-cone type).

Fig. 7.9. Hub bearing cone removed for bearing lubrication.

7

mended in Chapter 2. Ask the bike shop for the correct size for the wheel in question.

Procedure:

1. Remove the wheel, as de-scribed in Chapter 5.

2. While holding the cone firmly on one side with a cone wrench, loosen the locknut on the same side by about one full turn, using either an-other cone wrench or a regu-lar wrench.

3. Lift the keyed washer that's installed between the cone and the nut so it comes loose from the cone.
   • If the bearing was too loose, tighten the cone

about ⅛ turn at a time, while holding the locknut on the opposite side with a wrench.
   • If the bearing was too tight, loosen the cone about ⅛ turn at a time, while hold-ing the cone on the opposite side steady with another cone wrench.

5. Tighten the locknut, while holding the cone on the same side, then check the adjustment as described above and repeat the proce-dure, if needed, until the hub runs smoothly without side-ways play.

6. Reinstall the wheel in the bike, following the instruc-tions in Chapter 5.

Hub Lubrication

This is normally a job to leave to a bike mechanic. However, on a cup-and-cone bearing, you can do it in conjunction with the ad-justing procedure just described. Simply continue loosening the locknut and the cone of the bearing after Step 3 above. Then catch the bearing balls, clean ev-erything, and pack the bearings with bearing grease. Reassemble and adjust as described above.

CHAPTER 8

Drivetrain Maintenance

THE DRIVETRAIN comprises all the parts that transmit the rider's input to the rear wheel: crankset, chain, and pedals. The related gear change mechanisms will be treated separately in Chapters 9 and 10.

The Crankset

The crankset consists of the cranks, the bottom bracket

Fig. 8.1. Tightening or loosening the crank bolt (loosening shown).

(spindle and bearings), and the chainrings attached to the right-hand crank.

Most modern bicycles come equipped with a cotterless crankset. On these, the ends of the bottom bracket spindle are either tapered in a square pattern or splined, and the cranks are held on by means of a bolt (or sometimes a nut), which sits in a larger threaded cylindrical crank recess facing out, often with a dust cap over the bolt.

Older, and cheaper, bikes may have cranks that are attached by means of cotter pins.

Tighten Crank

Do this in conjunction with the monthly inspection, and whenever you notice creaking or other signs of looseness in the connection between the crank and the bottom bracket. The tool to use and the procedure to follow depends on the crank attachment detail as explained below.

Procedure for bikes with large exposed Allen bolt

1. Tighten the Allen bolt with an 8 mm Allen wrench, while

holding the crank firmly for leverage.

2. Also tighten the other crank, even if it did not seem loose.

Procedure for bikes with separate metal dust cap:

1. Remove the dust cap.

2. Using the wrench part of the crank tool, tighten the Bolt, while holding the crank firmly for leverage.

3. Reinstall the dust cap.

Remove and Install Crank

You may have to do this work to gain access to the bottom bracket itself, e.g., for bearing overhaul, or to replace the

Fig. 8.2. Splined crank and bottom bracket spindle.

crank, e.g., if it is bent or damaged.

Procedure:

1. Remove the dust cap and then the bolt — or, if it is an Allen bolt with a black plastic ring around it, just loosen the Allen bolt.

    If the bolt or the nut came out (square-spindle models), remove any washer that may be present (very important: if you forget this step, you won't be able to pull the crank off and perhaps ruin the screw thread in the crank).

    On splined-spindle models, just keep unscrewing the bolt, which will pull the crank off the spindle.

2. On models requiring use of the crank extractor tool, make sure there is no washer left in the recess and the puller is fully retracted; then screw it into the threaded recess in the crank as far as possible, using the wrench.

3. Holding the outer part of the crank extractor tool with one wrench, screw in the central part with the other one.

4. The crank will be pulled off this way; then unscrew the tool from the crank.

8

Installation procedure:

1. Clean and inspect, and, if necessary replace parts; then apply a thin layer of grease on the matching flat or splined surfaces of the bottom bracket spindle and the crank.

2. Place the crank on the bottom bracket spindle, 180 degrees offset from the other crank, and push it on by hand as far as possible.

3. On non-splined-spindle models, install the washer, then the bolt, and tighten the bolt firmly, using the crank for leverage.

4. Tighten the bolt and then, only on non-splined-spindle models, install the dust cap or the plastic ring.

5. After an hour's cycling, re-tighten the bolt; and once more after another 4 hours' use — and immediately any-time it seems to be getting loose (e.g., if you hear creaking sounds).

One-key crank attachment note:

If what looks like a dust cap around an 8 mm Allen bolt has two round recesses, it's probably the splined variety with a one-key release. On these, loosening the Allen bolt far enough actually pushes the crank off. Don't remove what looks like a dust cap.

Cottered crank procedure:

There are still some of these out there on older bikes, and they have to be maintained too. If a cottered crank comes loose, tighten it immediately to prevent more damage.

1. Support the crank close to the nut on the cotter pin on something solid, and hit the cotter pin from the other side with a mallet or a hammer; then tighten the nut.

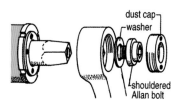

Fig. 8.3. One-key crank attachment detail.

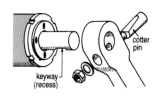

Fig. 8.4. Cottered crank attachment detail.

Bottom Bracket Maintenance

The bottom bracket is installed in the lowest point of the frame. The cranks are attached on either side. On modern bikes, it is usually a self-contained unit, or cartridge. Older bottom brackets, and those on some cheaper bikes, may have separate cup-and-cone bearings, known as BSA-type. In addition, there is the one-piece, or Ashtabula type, found on old American cruisers and children's bikes, and the Thompson type used on some low-end European bikes.

    Cartridge bottom bearings can not be adjusted, whereas each of the other types can. If you have a problem (loose or rough operation) with a cartridge bearing unit, have it serviced at the bike shop. The other types are serviced as described in the following sections.

Bottom Bracket Adjusting

This work can be done with the cranks still installed. You will need special tools, available from the bike shop.

Procedure:

1. Using the matching tool, unscrew the notched lockring on the left-hand side of the bottom bracket by about one turn.

2. Using the pin wrench of the bottom bracket tools, tighten or loosen the left-hand bearing cup about ⅛ turn.

3. Holding the bearing cup with the pin wrench, tighten the lockring firmly, making sure the bearing cup does not accidentally turn with it.

4. Check to make sure the adjustment is correct now and repeat, if necessary.

One-piece cranksets:

On this type, the two crank arms are combined, together with the spindle, as a single Z-shaped unit. They have to be adjusted

Fig. 8.5. Adjusting one-piece crank bottom bracket bearing.

about once a year, and whenever the bearing feels loose or tight.

Procedure:

1. Loosen the locknut on the left-hand side turning clockwise (left-hand thread).

2. Lift the keyed washer that lies underneath and then use the screwdriver to adjust the cone — to the left to tighten, to the right to loosen the bearing.

3. Holding the cone in place with the screwdriver, tighten the locknut counterclockwise.

Chainring Maintenance

In normal use, the chainrings last many years. On non-derailleur bikes, there's only one chainring, and it's often permanently attached to the right-hand crank, so it can only be replaced together with the crank.

If the chainring or its teeth are bent, get it (or them) straightened at a bike shop or replace the chainring.

Chainring tightening procedure:

The chainrings attachment has to be tightened if one or more of the installation bolts are loose,

which is also one of the possible causes for unpredictable shifting of derailleur gears.

Holding each of the bolts in the back of the chainring in turn with the slotted wrench, tighten the corresponding Allen bolt from the front, gradually working around until all bolts (usually four or five) have been tightened.

Chain Maintenance

The main things to consider are cleaning, lubrication, and the amount of wear (which leads to apparent "stretch"). With moderate use, a chain will last several years, as long as it remains well lubricated. To replace a worn chain, or to ease lubrication, you should know how to remove and

Fig. 8.6. Tightening chainring mounting bolts.

8

reinstall it. You'll need a chain tool, making sure it matches the specific chain on the bike.

Removal procedure:

1. Select the gear in which the chain runs over the smallest cog in the rear and the smallest chainring in the front.

2. Turn back the handle of the chain rivet tool (counter-clockwise), so the pin of the tool is retracted all the way. Then place the tool between two links, with the pin of the tool firmly up against the chain link pin.

3. Turn the handle in (clock-wise) firmly, pushing the chain link pin out; but don't

push the pin out all the way (it will be practically impossible to replace the pin if you push it out all the way) — just far enough so no more than 0.5 mm (about 1/32 in.) of the pin stays engaged.

4. Turn the handle back (counterclockwise) until it comes free of the chain, and remove the tool.

5. Wiggle the chain links apart at the point of the retracted chain link pin.

Installation procedure:

1. Select the gear by which the chain engages the smallest cog in the back and the smallest chainring in the front.

2. Working from the chain end that does not have the pin sticking out, wrap the chain around the chainring, through the front derailleur

Fig. 8.7. Use of chain tool.

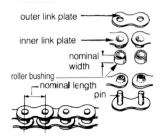

outer link plate
inner link plate
nominal width
roller bushing
nominal length
pin

Fig. 8.8. Chain details.

cage, around the small rear cog, and over and between the derailleur pulleys as shown in Fig. 5.4 (on page 29), until the two ends of the chain can be connected.

3. Place the slight inward protrusion of the pin that was pushed out over the inner link that forms the other end of the chain, and hold the two parts in place correctly aligned.

4. Turn the handle of the chain tool back far enough for the pin on the tool to clear the protruding end of the pin on the chain, and then turn it in until there is firm contact between the two pins.

5. While continuing to hold the two chain links properly aligned, turn the handle of the chain tool in, pushing the chain link pin in all the way until it protrudes equally far on both sides; then remove the tool.

6. Apply sideways force, twisting in both directions, until the two chain links around the newly replaced pin rotate freely. If it can't be done this way, put the chain tool on from the opposite side and push the chain link pin back in slightly.

General note:

If the pin is accidentally pushed all the way out during disassembly, you can remove the last two links and replace them with a new two-link section of chain — taking care not to lose the pin again.

Chain skip note:

If the chain skips off the cogs (usually only in the gear in which the smallest cog is engaged), it will be time to replace both the chain and that cog.

Chains with master link:

The wider chain used on many non-derailleur bicycles can be opened up and connected by means of the special master link provided with these chains. It is built up as shown in Fig. 8.9.

Remove it by prying off the spring clip with e.g., a small screwdriver (covering it with a cloth, so you don't lose the small spring). Then the loose link plate

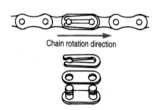

Chain rotation direction

Fig. 8.9. Detail of master link (non-derailleur bikes only).

8

49

can be lifted off and the rest of the link (the fixed link plate with the two pins attached) comes out from the other side of the chain. When installing a master link, make sure the direction of rotation of the chain is such that the closed end of the spring clip points forward in the direction of chain rotation.

If a non-derailleur chain is too loose or too tight (more or less than about ¾ inch, or 2 cm, up-and-down movement in the middle between chainring and cog), loosen the rear wheel and slide it back or forward, then retighten it. On a wheel with a hub brake, you'll have to loosen the counter lever and retighten it

in the right position once the wheel is installed.

Pedal Maintenance

The pedals are screwed into the threaded holes at the end of the cranks. The left-hand pedal has left-hand screw thread (and is usually marked with an "L"), while the right-hand pedal has regular right-hand screw thread. If you're having difficulty tightening or loosening a pedal, first check whether you're turning them the right way or not — left-hand thread means tighten counterclockwise and loosen clockwise.

Pedals come in two basic types — conventional and clipless. Clipless pedals always have cartridge bearings, while conventional pedals often have adjustable bearings.

Replacing Pedals

This work is required when the bike has to be stored in a small box, e.g., to be transported. Note that the pedal wrench may either be the metric size 15 mm or the non-metric size ⁹⁄₁₆ inch. Often, it can be done with an Allen wrench, instead.

Fig. 8.10. Tightening or loosening pedal using pedal wrench.

Removal procedure:

1. Place the pedal wrench on the flat surfaces of the stub between the pedal and the crank. (If the pedal is not on too tight, it can usually be done with the Allen wrench, reaching the hexagonal recess that's present in the end of most modern pedals from the back of the crank.)

2. Hold the crank arm firmly and:
   • for the right-hand pedal, turn counterclockwise;
   • for the left-hand pedal, turn clockwise.

3. Unscrew the pedal all the way.

Installation procedure:

1. Clean the thread surfaces in the cranks and on the pedals, and lubricate them lightly.

2. Align the thread of the pedal stub with the thread in the crank and start screwing it in by hand (counterclockwise for the left-hand pedal).

3. Screw in the pedal fully with the pedal wrench (or from the back of the crank, using the Allen wrench). There's no need to tighten them excessively.

Adjust Clipless Pedal Force

If it is too hard to get your foot out of a clipless pedal, or if it does not hold the shoe firmly enough, you can adjust the spring tension.

1. Locate the tension adjustment bolt or bolts on the pedal in question.

2. Tighten or loosen the bolt(s) as required.

3. Check operation and make fine-tuning adjustment, if necessary.

Adjust Pedal Bearings

This is only possible on conventional pedals with cup-and-cone bearings. It can be done without removing the pedals.

Fig. 8.11. Adjusting clipless pedal release force.

1. Holding the pedal at the crank, loosen the dust cap (it's usually threaded but may be snapped on, in which case you'll have to pry it off).

2. Unscrew the locknut by about one turn.

3. Using whatever tool fits the cone (a small screwdriver if the top of the cone is slotted), turn the cone in or out by about ¼ turn to tighten or loosen the bearing, respectively.

4. Holding the cone with the screwdriver, tighten the locknut.

5. Check the adjustment of the bearing and fine-tune the adjustment, if necessary, making sure the locknut is firmed up properly.

6. Reinstall the dust cap.

Lubricating procedure:

Much of this job requires the same work as described for adjusting, and only what's different will be listed here.

1. Follow Steps 1, 2, and 3 above, but remove locknut, washer, and cone all the way, catching the bearing balls with the cloth.

2. Pull the body off the spindle and catch the balls on the inside as well.

3. Clean everything and pack the bearing cups with grease, then reinsert the bearing balls and screw everything back together.

Fig. 8.12. The parts of an adjustable pedal (i.e. with cup-and-cone bearing).

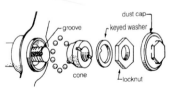

Fig. 8.13. Pedal bearing adjustment details.

8

4. Adjust the bearing as described above, then reinstall the dustcap.

Freewheel and Cog Maintenance

The rear wheel cogs are mounted on a freewheel mechanism, which is either integrated into a portion of the hub ("cassette hub") or in a separate unit that is screwed on to the hub ("freewheel block"). The cogs are either screwed on or held on splines and held together with a screwed-on item (either a separate lock ring or the smallest cog).

Occasionally, clean the cogs and the spaces between them. Remove the rear wheel (see Chapter 5). Then use a thin cloth, soaked in a mixture of solvent and 10% mineral oil, folded into a narrow strip, stretched between both hands, going back and forth all around.

The freewheel body can be lubricated with thick SAE 60 mineral oil inserted in the visible gap between moving parts inside. Do this with the wheel horizontal, catching the drips on the other side with a rag.

If the chain skips off the smallest cog, you'll have to replace the chain, as well as that cog.

Freewheel Removal

When a spoke on the chain side of the rear wheel breaks, you

Fig. 8.14. Removal of screwed-on freewheel block.

Fig. 8.15. Removal of cassette-type freewheel.

Fig. 8.16. Using the freewheel tool to disassemble a cassette.

Fig. 8.17. Cassette cog disassembly.

have to remove the freewheel or the cogs.

The screwed-on type is removed with a special freewheel tool: Remove the wheel, hold the tool loosely with the wheel's quick-release skewer, then unscrew it, using a large wrench, while holding the wheel firmly (loosen the quick-release thumb nut as needed along the way).

The cassette freewheel can be removed with a 10 mm Allen wrench as shown in Fig. 8.15. If it's a screwed-on type, clean and lubricate the screw thread, and screw the new freewheel on by hand. If it's a cassette, it is held on by means of a hollow internal 10 mm Allen bolt, accessible after you remove the spindle.

Replacing Cassette Cogs

1. With the wheel removed from the bike and held horizontally with the freewheel side up, use the freewheel manufacturer's cog tool and a matching Crescent wrench to unscrew the item on top (either a separate ring or the smallest cog).

2. Slide the cog(s) off the splined freewheel body.

3. Clean all parts and replace any worn or damaged cogs.

4. Reassemble in reverse order.

8

CHAPTER 9

Derailleur Gearing Maintenance

THE DERAILLEUR gearing system consists of a rear derailleur and a front derailleur, controlled by means of shifters to which the derailleurs are connected by means of gear control cables.

The rear derailleur selects one of 7 to 10 cogs on the rear freewheel with different numbers of teeth, and the front derailleur selects one of 2 or 3 different size chainrings in the front.

The shifters are either on the handlebars or on the frame's down tube. Road bikes are usually shifted by means of ratcheted levers integrated with the brake levers. Bikes with flat handlebars are either shifted by means of a rotating twist grip or by means of shift levers on the handlebars.

Think of derailleur gearing as a system, because if there is a problem, it may be due to any of a number of factors ranging from the derailleur mechanism to the cable to the shifter — in fact, even the chain or the cogs and chainrings may be at fault.

Over- and Undershift Adjustment

This is the most common derailleur problem: Either the highest or lowest gear cannot be reached (undershifting), or the chain is shifted beyond the smallest or biggest cog or chainring (oveshifting). It applies to the rear derailleur as well as the front derailleur.

Fig. 9.1. Rear derailleur range adjustment. The adjustment screws are marked "H" for high and "L" for low gear adjustment.

9

Procedure:

1. Find the two small adjusting screws that limit the sideways travel of the derailleur cage. Usually, one is marked "H" for high, limiting travel toward the high gear (outside, smallest cog or largest chainring), the other one "L" for low, limiting travel toward the low gear (inside, biggest cog or smallest chainring).

2. Turn the relevant adjusting screw in or out in ½-turn increments:
   • Turn the "H" screw in to compensate for overshifting at the high gear, or out to compensate for undershifting at the high end.

Fig. 9.2. Front derailleur range adjustment.

   • Turn the "L" screw in to compensate for overshifting at the low gear, or out to compensate for undershifting at the low end.

3. Lift the wheel off the ground and turn the crank, shifting into all the gears, and fine-tune the adjustment if necessary.

Adjust Front or Rear Derailleur

When the gears do not engage properly, first make sure the cable is in good condition (and have it replaced it if it isn't). Then proceed as follows to adjust:

Procedure:

1. Place the bike in an intermediate gear.

2. Locate the adjusting mechanism at the point where the control cable enters the derailleur.

3. Turn the adjuster out in ½-turn increments and try shifting through the entire range of gears, while turning the cranks with the wheel lifted off the ground. Note whether the problem gets better or worse.

- If the problem got better, continue adjusting in small increments until the derailleur indexes properly.
- If the problem got worse, turn the adjuster in the opposite direction until the derailleur indexes properly.

4. If you can't turn the adjuster in or out far enough:
- Use the additional adjuster at the shifter that may be present on bikes with flat handlebars.
- Select the highest gear, i.e., the smallest cog, then clamp the cable in at a different point with the wrench, using the needle-nose pliers to pull the cable taut.

5. If the highest or lowest gear cannot be reached properly, or the chain shifts beyond the gear, refer to *Over- and Undershift Adjustment* on page 55.

Angle adjustment note:

On the rear derailleur, there is usually an adjustment screw near the derailleur mounting point, to adjust the limiting angle of the derailleur cage. You may try adjusting this one way or the other, bringing the chain and the upper pulley (called "jockey pulley") closer to, or farther from, the cogs.

9

Fig. 9.3. Gear adjustment at rear derailleur.

Fig. 9.4. Gear adjustment at mountain bike-type shifter.

Fig. 9.5. Clamping in a gear control cable at the derailleur.

Replace Derailleur Cable

Replace the cable if its resistance is excessive. This may be due to corrosion or damage. Whether for the front or the rear derailleur, the procedure is the same. If it's an indexed derailleur, buy a cable for the particular derailleur on your bike; if not, just make sure it's a cable with the right type of nipple (check at the shifter what shape and size it has). Before you start, put the bike in the gear that engages the smallest cog in the rear or the smallest chainring in the front.

Procedure:

1. Undo the cable clamp bolt at the derailleur.

2. At the shifter, pull the cable housing back a little and then push the inner cable in toward the shifter to expose the nipple at the shifter and enough cable to reach that point with the pliers.

3. Pull the cable out, first with the pliers, then by hand, catching the various sections of cable housing at the shifter and (on a rear derailleur) at the derailleur.

4. Make sure the new cable and the cable housing sections are of the same type and length as the original. Then apply some lubricant to the inner cable.

5. Starting at the shifter, install the inner cable through the shifter, the cable housing sections, over or through any guides on the frame, and into the derailleur itself.

6. Clamp the cable end provisionally (not too tight yet).

7. Try the gears, turning the cranks with the wheel lifted off the ground, and adjust the cable (both with the adjuster and with the cable clamp bolt) until all gears work properly — refer to the preceding procedures *Adjust Rear Derailleur* and *Adjust Front Derailleur*.

CHAPTER 10

Hub Gearing Maintenance

ment. If you got one, refer to it, because the instructions there will be more specific to the make and model in question. If not, here are some tips to help you on your way.

USED MAINLY on utilitarian bikes and folders, a hub gearing system consists of a gear mechanism contained in a special hub in the rear wheel, a shifter mounted on the handlebars, and a control cable. Hubs are available with up to 8 different gearing stages.

Shifting is accomplished by a lever or a twist ring on the handlebars. One or more control cables connect the shifter with a selector mechanism on the side of the rear hub.

The gear hub is often combined with a hub brake, and their maintenance is covered in Chapter 12. To remove such a wheel from the bike for maintenance, you'll also have to disconnect the brake counter lever and the brake control cable, as well as the gear control cable itself — and install and adjust them again afterwards.

If bought new, these hubs should come with an instruction manual explaining their adjust-

Hub Gear Problems

When a hub gearing system does not work properly, it's usually something that can be alleviated with adjusting. If that doesn't do the job, you may well be faced with having to replace one of the system components — the shifter, the control cable, or the hub itself. Keeping the components clean and lightly lu-

10

Fig. 10.1. Adjustment of Sturmey-Archer three-speed hub gear.

bricated is your major line of defense against hub gear trouble.

Gear malfunctions usually show up as a failure to shift into one of the gears, at other times as failure to stay in a gear. Sometimes none of the gears can be engaged.

The first thing to try is simple adjusting. All hub gear systems come with an adjusting device either at the shifter or at the hub.

Adjusting Hub Gear

1. Set the shifter for the highest gear, while turning the cranks by hand with the rear wheel off the ground.

2. Check the cable where it attaches to the control mechanism at the hub: in the

selected position, the cable should be just slack, i.e., without tension. However, as soon as you shift down, the cable should become taut and the hub should engage the next gear as you move it to the next setting at the shifter.

3. If it doesn't shift properly, turn the adjuster in (to loosen) half a turn at a time and check whether the situation improves. If not, loosen it in similar increments.

SRAM note:

Instead of a conventional adjusting barrel, these have a "Click Box," with a spring clip, into which the threaded adjusting pin is pushed and held in place.

Fig. 10.2. Hub gear adjustment at shifter for Shimano hub gear.

Fig. 10.3. "Click Box" connector for SRAM hub gear control cable.

Easy to connect, to disconnect, and to adjust: just push the clip while pulling the threaded pin all the way out, then insert the pin again until the cable tension is right.

General note:

Sometimes the control that projects from the hub, which is in the form of a little chain (especially on older hubs) is either too loose or turned in under such an angle that the little chain is kinked. In the first case, undo the connection with the cable, and screw the control into the hub a little tighter; then reattach. In the second case, undo and loosen it a little so it is not kinked; then reattach.

Other Hub Gearing Maintenance

If the problem can't be alleviated with adjusting as described above, see what you can do with the following suggestions:

1. Clean and lightly lubricate all parts first — hub, cog(s), chain, control mechanism, cable, and shifter.

2. Check whether it really is a malfunction in the system itself: Make sure the chain is properly tensioned, the

Fig. 10.4. Lining up the color coded ring on a Shimano 7- or 8-speed hub.

wheel properly positioned, and the chainring and cog(s) engage the chain properly.

3. Next, check to make sure the cable is in good condition; free it if it is caught somewhere, lubricate it if it is dry, and replace it if it is kinked or frayed.

4. Loosen the control cable, and check whether the shifter works smoothly when it is not attached to the hub. If it doesn't, see what you can do to make it work, or replace it with a new one.

5. If the problem does not get resolved this way, it's time to ask around for a bike mechanic who knows how to deal with hub gears.

10

CHAPTER 11

Rim Brake Maintenance

MOST BICYCLES are equipped with one of two versions of the rim brake: Mountain bikes usually come with V-brakes, while road bikes are usually equipped with sidepull brakes. Older bikes may have other types of rim brakes. And there are hub and disk brakes, which are covered in Chapter 12.

Common Rim Brake Features

There are a couple of aspects that all rim brakes have in com-

mon, and these are the first, and most general, points to pay attention to when checking or maintaining the brakes.

All rim brakes have two brake pads that are pressed inward against the sides of the wheel rim. To achieve that, you pull a lever on the handlebars, which is connected to the brake mechanism by means of a flexible cable.

Adjustability is provided either at the point where the cable comes out of the lever or at the point where the cable connects to the brake mechanism. Somewhere in the system is usually a quick-release device or some easily handled method of unhooking the inner cable or the outer cable housing.

The most common adjustments are those of the brake

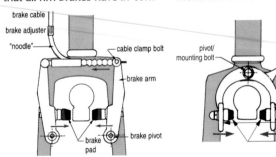

Fig. 11.1. V-brake

Fig. 11.2. Sidepull brake

pad position relative to the rim and the cable tension. The former adjustment assures that the brake pad wears evenly and works fully when engaged; the latter adjustment determines how quickly and powerfully it can be engaged.

When working on the brakes, treat them as complete systems, which include not only the brakes themselves, but also the levers, the cables, and any attachments through which the cables run. Even the condition of the wheel rim influences brake performance.

Brake Adjustments

When the brake works inadequately, it can probably be fixed by means of adjusting. The following sections contain summaries of the various procedures to improve the performance of the brake. Before you proceed with adjustments, first check the condition of the rim and the brake pads. Clean them (the rims with solvent, the pads with sandpaper) if needed.

Adjust Brake Application

Over time, brake pad wear, cable stretch, and pivot bushing wear

in the various components combine to make the point where the brake lever activates the brake to get closer and closer to the point where the lever gets too close to the handlebars to apply sufficient force. It must be adjusted if it no longer applies powerful braking force when it is ¾ inch (2 cm) from the handlebars.

Procedure:

1. Find the adjuster. On road bikes with sidepull brakes, it's usually on the brake arm to which the cable housing is anchored. On mountain bike brakes, it's usually on the brake lever at the point where the cable housing

Fig. 11.3. Brake adjustment on sidepull brake.

comes out of the lever body.

Establish what kind of adjuster it is. On most modern road bikes, it's the type without a locknut. On older bikes it may be the type with a locknut.

2. Also find the cable quick-release, which on most road bike brakes is on the brake arm where the inner cable is clamped in. On V-brakes, it's the bent piece of metal tubing that guides the cable housing between the brake arms — to use it, squeeze the brake arms together at the top and wiggle that tube out from the bracket that holds it at the bottom. Don't do anything yet.

3. Depending on the type of adjuster:

Fig. 11.4. Brake cable adjustment on mountain bike brake.

• If you're working on a bike with the adjuster without locknut, first use the quick-release to untension the cable. Then turn the adjuster in about one turn (to tighten) or out (in case you want the brake to grab later than it does now). Then tighten the quick-release again, check and repeat, if necessary.

• If you're working on a bike with an adjuster with a locknut (usually the case on all mountain bike brakes and on older bikes of any type), proceed as follows:

4. Loosen the locknut by several turns, which can usually be done by hand, without the need for a tool.

5. Turn the adjusting barrel relative to the part into which it is screwed (to loosen) or out (to tighten) the tension on the cable. Loosening will open up the brake; tightening will do the opposite.

6. Holding the adjusting barrel with one hand, tighten the locknut again, then check and repeat, if necessary.

7. If you run out of adjusting range, the cable has to be clamped in at a different point:

• Release the cable tension with the quick-release (or un-hook the cable) and then loosen the adjuster as far as possible (after unscrewing the locknut, if present).

• Loosen the bolt or the nut that clamps the end of the inner cable at one of the brake arms (or, in the case of cantilever and centerpull brakes, the particular location where the main cable ends) by about one full turn.

• With the needle-nose pliers, pull the cable about 3/8 inch (1 cm) further in and tighten the bolt or the nut again.

8. Tighten the adjuster (and the locknut, if provided) about ¼ of the way, then tighten the quick-release and check operation of the brake — and repeat Step 6.

Adjusting Brake Pads

Make this correction if the brake test or any other inspection revealed that the brake pads do not lie flat and straight on the side of the rim with about 1/16 inch (1–2 mm) clearance to the tire when the brake lever is pulled in.

Procedure:

1. Holding the brake pad with one hand, undo the bolt or the nut that holds it to the brake arm by about one turn — just enough to allow controlled movement into the right position.

2. While applying the brake lever so the brake pad is pushed up against the rim, twist the brake pad into the appropriate orientation and hold it firmly in place there.

3. While holding the brake pad firmly, let go of the brake lever (unless you have an assistant to do that for you) use the free hand to tighten the bolt or the nut that holds the brake pad to the brake arm.

Fig. 11.5. Brake pad adjustment.

11

4. Check to make sure both brake pads are properly aligned now and make any corrections necessary, then retighten.

Brake Centering

This work is required if one brake pad touches the rim before the other one, especially if it rubs on the surface of the rim while riding.

Depending on the type of brake, you may be able to find one or more small grub screws that point in vertically from the top (on a dual-pivot sidepull brake) or sideways at the pivots. Check what happens if you tighten or loosen these screws. Adjust them until the brake works symmetrically, if possible.

Then make sure the brake is still working properly in other ways and make any final adjustments that may be needed.

If there is no such screw, or if the desired result cannot be obtained, you may have to rotate the entire brake a little (usually the case on older caliper brakes). Do that either with a small thin wrench that fits two flat surfaces on the mounting bolt on many sidepull brakes. Otherwise, undo the mounting bolt, realign the entire brake and hold it steady there, applying force at the lever; then tighten the mounting bolt again.

On V- and cantilever brakes, the asymmetrical action may be due to uneven spring tension at the brake arms. To correct that, remove the brake arms, and ei-

Fig.11.6. Centering a single-pivot sidepull brake.

Fig. 11.7. Centering a modern dual-pivot sidepull brake.

ther hook one or both of the springs into a different hole on the mounting plate (if provided) on the pivot boss — or use pliers to tension one of the springs more. Then reassemble the brake arms, check operation of the brake, and make any other adjustments that may be needed.

Brake Squeal and Rumble

Sometimes, brakes are noisy when applied. They may make either a squealing or a rumbling sound. Before trying to adjust anything, once more make sure the rim and the brake pads are clean. Here's the way to eliminate these noises.

Brake squeal procedure:

Usually, adjusting is all you have to do to eliminate these noises. If the brake pads so that the front part (the "trailing edge") of the pad touches the rim when the rear is still 2 mm (3/32 inch) away from the rim. This condition is referred to as "toed in." If this does not do the trick, also try it the other way round, the back touching the rim first instead.

Brake rumble procedure:

If cleaning the rim and the brake pad did not solve the problem, it's usually because something is loose, and you'd better tighten it. First suspect is the brake itself. Check the mounting bolts of the brakes and the individual brake arms and all related pivot points. However, sometimes it's another part of the bike that's loose — most typically the headset (see Chapter 13).

Replacing Brake Cable

If operating the brake seems to require excessive force despite poor braking, the problem is probably due to the cable. It may be kinked, dirty or corroded, or

Fig. 11.8. Clamping in the brake cable on a V-brake.

11

there may be broken strands. Inspect the cable for obvious signs of damage. Replace it if cleaning and lubrication does not alleviate the problem. Buy a replacement cable of at least the same length, making sure it has the same type of nipple. In addition to the regular tools, it will be best to use cable cutters (or ask the bike shop to cut the cable).

Procedure:

1. Undo the bolt or the nut that clamps in the cable at the brake.

2. Pull the brake lever and let go again while restraining the cable to loosen the cable. For aero-brake levers (with hidden cables), use the

needle-nose pliers to grab the end of the cable near the nipple inside the brake lever, and pull enough cable free to get at it by hand to remove the rest of the inner cable. Also catch any sections of cable housing that were used and any ferrules that went around the end of the cable housing where it was held at anchor points.

• On mountain bike brake levers, the brake cable can usually be lifted out easily once you turn the adjuster and the locknut into such an orientation that the grooves that are cut into both parts line up with a cutout in the brake mounting bracket.

• If there seems to be a kink in a section of cable housing

Fig. 11.9. Pull the lever to gain access to the cable nipple insertion point on a road bike.

Fig. 11.10. Replacing brake cable at mountain bike lever.

that lies under the handlebar tape on a road bike, remove the handlebar tape, replace that piece of cable housing and rewrap the handlebars.

3. Apply some lubricant (wax or grease on a cloth) to the new inner cable before installing it.

4. Depress the brake lever and find the place where the cable nipple is held, then insert the cable (you may need to wiggle and twist the innards of the lever a little at the point where the nipple is held to do that).
   • On mountain bike brake levers, the brake cable can usually be installed at the lever by turning the adjuster and the locknut into such an orientation that the slots cut into both parts line up with the cutout in the brake mounting bracket.

5. Route the inner cable through the various sections of cable housing and cable stops (making sure to install the ferrules at the points where the cable housing ends at the cable stops, the brake, and the lever).

6. Clamp the end of the inner cable in at the termination point on the brake while pull-

Fig. 11.11. Hydraulically operated rim brake

ing it taut with the needle-nose pliers.

7. Make a provisional adjustment of the brake tension and then test the brake operation, making any final adjustments.

Hydraulic Rim Brakes

Rare enough not to discuss in great detail here, hydraulically operated rim brakes should at least be mentioned here. Since hydraulic operation is far more common for disk brakes than it is for rim brakes, maintenance of hydraulic systems will be described in Chapter 12.

11

Maintenance of Other Brakes

S OME BRAKES don't work at the rim but at the center of the wheel. Disk brakes, coaster brakes, drum brakes, and roller brakes all fall into this category, and their maintenance is covered in this chapter

You'll be shown the common adjustments to carry out if any of these brakes works poorly. If adjusting doesn't do the trick, it's time to take the bike into the shop for brake overhaul or replacement.

What all these brakes have in common is that the wheel's rotation is retarded by a friction mechanism installed at the hub, while a stationary part is held fixed to the bike frame or fork.

Brake Adjustment

Except for the coaster brake, all brakes of this type can be adjusted by means of a device similar to the one found on rim brakes. Consequently, you are referred to the relevant steps in the description *Brake Adjustments* in Chapter 11.

Fig. 12.1. Typical modern roller-type hub brake for the rear

Fig. 12.2. Disk brake, showing attachment to front fork.

Cable and Lever Maintenance

Also this operation is similar to what was described in Chapter 11 for rim brakes, both for the cable and the lever. Refer to the relevant procedures in that chapter.

Attachment Problems

The fixed portion of disk brakes is bolted directly to the fork or the frame. All other hub brakes have a counterlever, which must be firmly attached to the left-hand chainstay or fork blade. Check the mounting bolt(s) from time to time, and tighten, if necessary.

This is also a part that will have to be loosened in order to remove the wheel — and tightened again properly upon reinstallation of the wheel. If it is not bolted directly to a welded-on plate on the frame or the fork, you should make sure this clamp fits properly — if it can't be tightened properly, wrap something around the tube where the clamp goes, so that all slack is taken up. You can use a strip cut from an old inner tube for this purpose.

If a drum brake was added as an aftermarket item on a bike

not designed for it, the counter lever force may bend the frame tube or fork blade. Check to make sure that your hub brake is not bending the fork or the chain stays — and let the bike shop deal with it.

Disk Brake Maintenance

First used only on downhill mountain bikes, they are now making inroads in the field of more mundane uses. This section deals with their basic maintenance, including the issues relating to hydraulic operation.

Disk Problems

The disk is usually attached to the (special) hubs by means of

Fig. 12.3. Rear hub brake counter lever attachment detail.

Fig. 12.4. Tightening disk-to-wheel attachment bolts on disk brake.

shallow-headed Allen bolts or Torx bolts (similar to Allen bolts but with a star-shaped recess instead of a hexagonal one). Use a fitting Allen or Torx wrench to make sure they are properly tightened.

Keep hydraulic liquid and other oils away from the disk, and clean any oil, dirt, or brake pad deposits with rubbing alcohol. If the disk drags on the calipers, it's not corrected by anything you do to the disk but by moving the calipers in or out a little (see below).

Caliper Maintenance

The calipers are attached to standardized bosses attached to the frame at the rear dropout and to the back of the front fork.

They're held in place with 6 mm Allen bolts, and they too must be kept firmly tightened.

Never apply the brake lever when the wheel (with the disk) is removed from the bike. This would make the brake pads bind together, making it hard to separate them. To prevent this, insert the plastic protector plate that came with the brake unit between the pads.

The disk should run exactly in the middle between the brake pads. Turn the adjusting bolts on both sides of the calipers in or out to adjust the pad location.

Turn the pad adjuster (accessible from the side) in to adjust the pads when needed. Clean the pads with a piece of emery cloth twice a year or whenever the brakes squeal.

Hydraulic System Maintenance

This note apply to all hydraulic disk brakes — whether disk or caliper brakes. If the brakes feel "spongy," you'll have to bleed the system, i.e. let air bubbles out. At least once a year, you should flush all the oil out and replace it with fresh oil from time to time. It's a job best left to the bike shop.

12

CHAPTER 13

Steering System Maintenance

THE STEERING system comprises the handlebars, the stem, the front fork, and the headset bearings. Depending whether the bike has front suspension or not, the fork is covered in Chapter 14 or 16.

The Handlebars

The handlebars are connected to fork via the stem, one end of which is clamped to the front fork's steerer tube and the other around the center portion of the handlebars.

There are drop handlebars (used on road bikes) and flat handlebars (used on all other bikes). Drop bars get wrapped with handlebar tapes, while handgrips are used on flat bars.

The clamp with which the handlebars are connected with the stem is held by means of one or two Allen bolts. How the stem attaches to the fork's steerer tube depends on the type of headset used:

- On bikes with a conventional threaded headset, the stem is held in the fork's steerer tube by means of a wedge (or sometimes a conical item) that in turn is clamped in with a binder bolt reached from the top of the stem.

- On bikes with a threadless headset, the stem is clamped around an extension of the fork's steerer tube that sticks out above the upper headset.

Fig. 13.1. The steering system.

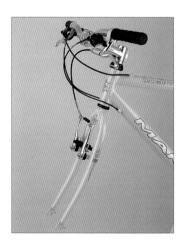

13

Adjust Handlebar Height

This simplest of all handlebar adaptations only works on bikes with a conventional threaded headset (on bikes with a thread-less headset, the only way to raise or lower the handlebars is by means of installing a different stem).

Procedure:

1. Clamp the front wheel be-tween your legs from the front and loosen the binder bolt on top of the stem by about 5 turns.

2. Tap on the bolt with a mallet (or a hammer, protecting the bolt with a block of wood) to loosen the wedge inside the stem — the bolt will drop down, loosening the stem.

3. Raise or lower the handle-bars as desired and hold them there firmly.

4. Check to make sure the marking that shows the max-imum extension of the stem does not show above the headset.

5. Holding the handlebars at the desired height and straight (still clamping the front wheel between your

Fig. 13.3. Holding the front wheel clamped in while working on the steering system.

Fig. 13.2. Adjusting handlebar height on bike with threaded headset.

legs), tighten the bolt on top of the stem firmly.

Note:

At least 2½ inches (6.5 cm) of the stem must remain clamped in. Usually, the stem is marked for this insertion depth, but even if it's not, that's the minimum for safety.

Adjust Handlebar Angle

Especially for drop handlebars, this adjustment allows you to find a more comfortable rotation of the handlebars, if needed.

Procedure:

1. Undo the clamp bolt(s) that hold the stem clamp around the handlebars by about one turn.

2. Turn the handlebars into the desired orientation, making sure they remain centered on the stem.

3. Holding the bars in the desired orientation and location, tighten the stem clamp bolt(s).

Replace Handgrips

Do this if the old grips (on a bike with flat handlebars) are not comfortable — or if you have to replace the brake lever, the gear shifter, the handlebars, or the stem.

Procedure:

1. Remove the old handgrips by pulling and twisting — if they do not come off easily, place the screwdriver under the old grip and let some dishwashing liquid enter between the grip and the handlebars. If all else fails, cut the grip lengthwise and "peel" it off.

2. Push the new handgrips over the ends of the handlebars. If

Fig. 13.4. Loosening bolts holding stem on a threadless headset.

13

they don't go on easily, soak them in warm water first. To make them adhere better, you can spray some hair spray inside the grips just before installing them.

Handlebar Extensions

Handlebar extensions (also called "bar-ends"), are forward-pointing extensions that can be installed at the ends of flat mountain bike handlebars to offer the rider an additional riding position. They are clamped around the ends of the handlebars. Here are some relevant notes.

- Since these things may form a hazard in a fall if they stick straight out, protect their ends with a rounded plug.

Fig. 13.5. Adjusting threaded headset bearing.

- Tighten their attachment clamp bolts once a month.

- Adjust them so they point forward and up by 15 to 30 degrees. To change the angle, loosen the clamp bolts, twist them, and retighten the bolts.

The Headset

The headset consists of an upper and a lower set of ball bearings, mounted in the top and the bottom of the frame's head tube, respectively. Two different types of headsets are in common use on modern bikes:

- The conventional bearing has a screw-threaded adjustable bearing race that is screwed onto the fork's steerer tube.

- The threadless headset, which is adjusted from the top of the handlebar stem.

Comparing the illustrations will help you define which type is installed on your bike.

Adjust Threaded Headset

If the bearings are too tight or too loose, first try to adjust them. If that does not solve the problem, you'll have to proceed to the instructions for overhauling, or even replacing, the headset.

Procedure:

1. Loosen the locknut on top of the upper headset bearing about one turn. If the locknut is held with a grub screw, loosen it before trying to undo the locknut.

2. Lift the keyed washer that lies under the locknut to allow the adjustable bearing race to be rotated.

3. Turn the adjustable bearing face in 1/8-turn increments (clockwise to tighten, counterclockwise to loosen) until it feels just barely loose (that slack will get taken up when the locknut is screwed down).

4. Tighten the locknut fully, while holding the adjustable race with the other wrench.

5. Check to make sure the bearing is properly adjusted now, or fine-tune the adjustment, if necessary, then tighten the locknut firmly. If there is a grub screw, tighten it.

Figs. 13.6. Adjusting threadless headset bearing.

Adjust Threadless Headset

The threadless headset tends to stay properly adjusted longer, but there may still be a need for adjustment from time to time.

Procedure:

1. Loosen the clamp bolts that hold the stem around the fork's steerer tube by about one turn each.

2. Tighten or loosen the Allen bolt on top of the stem. Tighten by turning the bolt clockwise, loosen by turning it counterclockwise.

3. When the adjustment feels right, tighten the stem clamp bolts, making sure the handlebars are straight.

13

CHAPTER 14

Frame & Fork Maintenance

THE FRAME together with the front fork are referred to as the frameset. The kind of damage that these parts are likely to sustain is either so minor that it doesn't really matter much (e.g., scratched paint) or so major that it can't be fixed, requiring replacement instead. That's why this chapter mainly deals with checking for damage, rather than actually fixing things. The one thing you can do — at least on a frame made of steel or welded aluminum — is touch up damaged paint, which will be covered here.

Frame Inspection

If the bike has been in a fall or collision, check it over thoroughly. If there are signs of bending, buckling, or cracking, take it to a bike shop and ask what you should do.

The two most significant parts to watch out for are the front fork and the area of the down tube just behind the lower headset. If you see any bulging or cracking, check with the bike shop. If there is no obvious damage, check for distortion of frame and fork, as per the following procedures.

14

Fig. 14.1. Frame and fork. The two main parts are connected by means of the headset (the threaded variety, in this photo of a hand-built touring frame).

Fork Inspection

What matters here is the alignment of the two fork blades relative to each other and relative to the steerer tube. On a regular fork, you can usually check the alignment by means of a visual inspection.

Procedure:

1. Place the fork flat on the level surface, supporting it at the fork crown and the upper straight section of the fork blades.

2. Compare the distance between the level surface and the fork ends. If there's a difference, they're misaligned.

3. Visually establish whether the line that goes through the center of the steerer tube also goes through the center of the upper straight portion of the fork blades. If it doesn't, you have misalignment between the fork blades and the steerer tube.

4. Also in this case, once you have established that there is misalignment, go to a bike shop and get advice on what to do.

Paint Touch-Up

If the paint comes off parts of a regular painted, brazed or welded metal frame or fork, you can touch up the paint to prevent rust and to keep the bike looking as nice as possible. Don't do this on carbon fiber

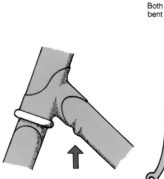

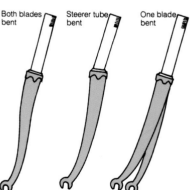

Both blades bent   Steerer tube bent   One blade bent

Fig. 14.2. Typical downtube damage due to collision.

Fig. 14.3. Typical fork damage misalignment.

14

frames, nor on a frame with bonded joints, because the solvents used either in preparation or actual painting may weaken the epoxy, possibly voiding the warranty. You'll need matching paint, a small brush, paint thinner, fine sandpaper, and a clean dry cloth.

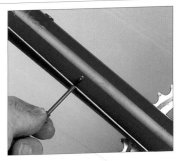

Fig. 14.4. Paint touch-up.

Procedure:

1. Thoroughly clean the area of (and around) the damage.

2. Use an emery cloth or a tiny speck of steel wool to remove corrosion, dirt, and paint remnants down to the bare, shiny metal surface in the damaged spot.

3. Clean the spot to be repainted once more with a cloth soaked in paint thinner, and wipe it dry.

4. Shake the paint thoroughly to mix it well.

5. Using the tiny brush, just barely dipped in paint, apply paint only to the damaged area.

6. Let it dry for at least 24 hours, and repeat Steps 4 and 5, if necessary.

14

CHAPTER 15

Seat & Seatpost Maintenance

T HE SEAT is held on the bike by means of a tubular seatpost, which is clamped in at the seat lug, at the top of the seat tube. The seat lug is tightened around the seatpost, either with a bolt or with a quick-release. Refer to Chapter 16 if the bike has a suspension seatpost.

Adjust Seat Height

Once you've determined how high you want the seat to be, this is how you get it there.

Procedure:

1. Depending on the type of seat clamp:
    • On a bike with a regular bolted clamp, undo the bolt (referred to as binder bolt) by 2–3 turns.
    • On a bike with quick-release clamp, twist the quick-release lever into the "open" position.

2. Try to move the seatpost up or down in a twisting move-ment, using the seat for le-

Figs. 15.1. Seat and seatpost.

Figs. 15.2. Adjusting the seat height.

15

verage and holding the bike's frame. If it doesn't budge, squirt some penetrating oil in at the point where the seat lug is slotted. Wait 2–3 minutes and try again.

3. Move it to the exact location where you want it to be, but make sure the marker that shows the minimum insertion depth is not exposed (if it is, it'll be dangerous to ride that way, and you'll need either a longer seatpost or a bigger frame).

4. Holding the seat at the right height and straight, tighten the binder bolt or the quick-release. (If the quick-release can't be tightened properly, flip it to "open" again, adjust the thumb nut, and try again.)

5. Check to make sure the position is correct, and if not, fine-tune the adjustment.

Notes:

1. You may find that you now need to adjust the angle and forward position in accordance with the instructions below as well.

2. At least 2½ inches (6.5 cm) of the seatpost must be clamped in. Usually the seatpost is marked to show this minimum safe insertion depth.

Adjust Angle and Forward Position

These features are adjusted by means of one or more bolts, accessible from under the seat,

Fig. 15.3. Seat angle adjustment on a high-end bike.

Fig. 15.4. Simple seat clip on a low-end bike.

15

Fig. 15.5. Tensioning leather seat.

that hold the seat wires to the seatpost.

Procedure:

1. Identify the bolts in question; usually they're easily accessible from below, but they can be tricky to get at on old seats (between the seat cover and the clamp). On low-end bikes there's one nut on either side of the wires (or the flat rails often used on such seats).

2. Loosen the bolt(s) — usually there are two — about 3 turns.

3. Move the seat forward or backward on the wires (while making sure the clamp remains on the wires) and hold it at the desired location under the desired angle.

4. Holding the seat steadily in place, tighten the bolts — gradually tightening both of them in turn if there are two.

5. Check to make sure the position is correct, and fine-tune the adjustments, if necessary.

Maintenance of Leather Seat

The thick leather seat covers used on some high-end bikes may stretch over time, especially if they get wet. Keep it dry and treat the cover with leather grease once or twice a year. Let it sit overnight so it penetrates properly before using the seat. Once a year, you may have to tension the seat cover to compensate for stretch.

Tightening procedure:

1. Look under the seat cover near the tip, and identify the bolt that holds the tip of the seat cover to the wires, then find the nut on this bolt for adjusting.

2. Tighten the nut about ½ turn at a time until the seat cover has the right tension. Do not overtighten.

15

CHAPTER 16

Suspension Maintenance

NOT ONLY mountain bikes, but even commuter bicycles often come with some form of suspension these days.

The three most important measures of suspension are travel (the difference between the compressed and uncompressed state), preload (the force on the spring when inactive),

Fig. 16.1. Typical modern full-suspension bike.

and stiction (resistance to initial movement)

For rough terrain, you want more travel and stiction than for a bike ridden mainly on relatively smooth paths. Preload should be no more than 25 percent of travel. Most systems have adjustments for preload, while the other features are given for any suspension unit.

Suspension Stems

This is the simplest way of adding front suspension. This device takes the place of a regular stem holding the handlebars. You can adjust its spring rate by tightening or loosening an Allen bolt to pre-tension the spring element.

Suspension Seatposts

These are also effective low-budget devices for smoothing out the ride on a bike intended for an upright rider position.

Here too, preload is the only factor that can be adjusted on the suspension seatpost. To do that, remove the seatpost from the bike, as described in Chapter 15, and use an Allen wrench to tighten or loosen the preload adjuster plug in the bottom of the seatpost — turning it in tightens the initial compression of the spring element inside; turning it out slackens it. For the sake of safety, don't unscrew it so far that any part of the adjuster plug extends from the seatpost.

Suspension Fork Maintenance

A suspension fork incorporates two sets of tubes that slide inside each other, the inner ones (the stanchion tubes) being guided in the outer ones (called slider tubes) and connected with spring elements. The spring elements are either elastomer pads, metal coil springs, or air cartridges.

Keep the seals and the stanchion tubes clean. Do this once a month and after every ride in wet weather or dusty terrain. Wipe the exposed parts of the stanchions and the seals; then apply synthetic oil to these parts and push the fork in five times; then wipe the stanchion tubes off once more.

In addition, check the suspension fork at least once a season to make sure it is working properly, as described below.

Checking procedure:

1. Holding the bike firmly at the headset, try to wiggle the bottom of the fork at the

Fig. 16.2. Adjusting a suspension stem.

Fig. 16.3. Adjusting suspension seatpost once removed from the frame.

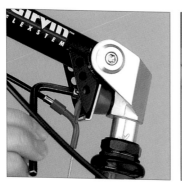

16

fork-ends. If they move loosely, you have a problem, which you should refer to a bike shop mechanic.

2. Holding the bike from the front at the handlebars, push down with all your body weight and observe how the suspension fork reacts. If all is well, it goes down with increasing resistance but does not stop suddenly.

3. With the suspension fork pushed in as in Step 2, release pressure and observe whether the recovery is smooth and quick.

4. If any of the criteria above are not met, you may have a problem, and it's recommended you refer it to a bike shop.

Travel and preload adjustment:

Referring to the information supplied with the fork in question, locate the preload adjuster (usually on top of each stanchion). Turn it to reduce the preload to the lowest value. Then check the ride to see whether it bottoms out on rebound. If it does, adjust the preload up a little. This will give you the maximum amount of effective travel.

Rear Suspension Maintenance

Even rear suspension is now penetrating other market seg-

Fig. 16.4. Preload adjustment on a typical suspension fork.

Fig. 16.5. Keep the rear suspension pivot points lubricated.

Fig. 16.6. After cleaning the stanchions, apply special non-sticky lubricant. Also applies to rear shock units.

ments besides downhill mountain bikes. There are numerous variations, but they all have a shock unit and one or more pivot points between the frame and the part that holds the rear wheel.

From a maintenance standpoint, there are two important things to watch, and they're common on all types: the shock unit itself and the pivots.

If you don't want to get more involved, as described below, at least keep all these parts clean, and lightly lubricate the pivot points regularly, using a non-greasy lubricant, such as a wax-based one, or even WD-40. Wipe off any excess lubricant. Also tighten the pivot bolts once a month.

Shock Unit Maintenance

The heart of any rear suspension system is a shock unit, comprising the spring element and a damping device. The spring element may be an external coil spring or a discretely hidden air cartridge. The damping device is usually an oil cylinder with valves through which the oil flows as the piston is displaced.

In addition to regularly cleaning the shock unit once a month and after each ride in wet or dusty terrain, inspect the unit once a month. If there are any traces of oil, it means the unit leaks, and it must be replaced by a bicycle mechanic.

16

CHAPTER 17

Accessory Maintenance

A N ACCESSORY is any part that is, or can be, installed on the bike but is not part of its essential operation. In this chapter, we'll deal with the most important accessories.

General Accessory Comments

The two tenets of accessory maintenance are:

Fig. 17.1. Keep the mounting hardware for accessories tightened.

- keep them properly mounted
- replace or remove what's broken

Check the installation hardware regularly, tightening all nuts, bolts, and clamps. And by all means, remove the item if it doesn't work and you haven't been able to fix it. Before replacing it in that case, ask yourself whether you could do without it.

Any attachment hardware should have at least two mounting bolts. Another thing to watch out for is that items clamped around another part of the bike should fit snugly. It's best to install a flexible plastic or rubber protective sleeve inside the clamp.

Lights

There are three types of lighting for the bike:
- Lights with internal batteries
- Lights with central batteries
- Generator lights

The following sections contain detailed maintenance information on all available types of lighting systems.

Lights with Internal Batteries

In the front, these usually clamp directly or indirectly on to the handlebars. In the rear, they attach either to the seatpost or e.g., to a luggage rack or the seat stays. The one used for the front should be bright and produce a compact bundle of light that should be aimed at an area of the road about 20–30 feet (6–9 m) in front of the bike.

The rear light should be red, and point straight back (neither up nor down, neither left nor right). It does not need to be quite so bright as the one in front. LEDs (Light Emitting Diodes) are very suitable for this use, mainly because they pro-vide much longer battery life. The LEDs themselves also last much longer than light bulbs — however, they don't last forever either, and the light will have to be replaced if they become dim.

The most common maintenance required on battery lights is replacing the batteries and the bulbs. A battery charge typically lasts less than 4 hours, so carry spares. Before you go on a longer ride that may take you in the evening, check the condition of both the batteries in the light and the spare batteries.

Light bulbs typically don't last more than about 100 hours of use. Buy some spare bulbs and carry one for each light on the bike, e.g., in the tire patch kit. If you use the nice bright halogen bulbs, don't touch the glass with your bare hands.

Fig. 17.2. Simple front light with internal battery.

Fig. 17.3. LED rear light with the red lens removed.

Lights with Central Battery

These lights are typically more powerful and often have high beam and low beam capabilities. Their larger battery, consisting of several cells wired up together, are either packaged in a pouch tied to the bike or neatly packed away in something that fits in a water bottle cage.

Again, the batteries and the bulbs need to be checked and replaced, if necessary (although the batteries are almost always rechargeable, in which case you just plug the unit in via its re-charging adapter, which should do the trick in about 2 hours).

In addition to bulbs and batteries, there is wiring to deal with. So, if the light doesn't work and you've checked the bulb

and the battery, and found them to be OK, check the wiring. Usually it's a connection at the end of the wiring, so check there first and fix the connection, preferably with a soldering iron and solder. If there are any exposed metal wire parts, use electrical insulating tape to fix it. You may have to replace the wiring completely if you can't identify the source of the problem.

Generator Lights

This type also has a central power source and wiring connecting it to the light(s) — the generator usually feeds both a front light and a rear light. The

Fig. 17.4. Wiring connector on a typical light with central battery.

Fig. 17.5. On this front-wheel-mounted generator light, the front light mounts to the same bracket as the generator.

electricity is carried by a single wire and returned to the generator via the metal of the bike, for which purpose each part — generator, front light, and rear light — has a pinch-screw to make what's called a "mass contact."

The most common problem, other than burned-out bulbs, is wiring failure. Especially the point where the wires connect to the dynamo is subject to accidental disconnection. Check it frequently and be careful to route your wire so that it isn't likely to get caught when e.g., storing or parking the bike.

Systematic Troubleshooting

If a lighting system with central battery or generator does not work properly, proceed systematically to find out what's wrong. Follow the steps outlined in diagram Fig. 17.6.

For lights with a central battery, keep the battery fully charged. Consider carrying a small light with built-in batteries as a spare light source.

Generators often slip in wet weather. The problem can be minimized by bending the

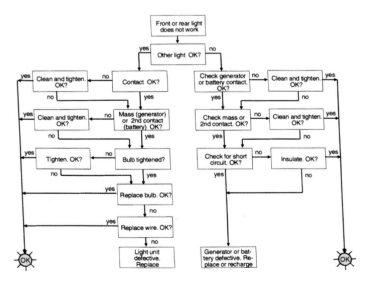

Fig. 17.6. Troubleshooting diagram for systems with central electric source.

mounting hardware in to the point where the unengaged position leaves only about ¼ in. (6 mm) between the roller and the tire. You can also place a rubber cap around the roller.

Bottom-bracket mounted models are most notorious for slipping. On those, tie a little bungee cord between the roller mount and a fixed point on the bike close to the rear wheel axle.

Hub generators, finally, are built into the front wheel, and aren't subject to slipping.

Reflectors

Make sure that front and rear reflectors are mounted facing oncoming traffic, and adjust if necessary. Replace any reflector that is cracked or broken, because water can enter through the crack and "fog up" the reflective pattern on the inside of the lens, making it "blind."

Lock

Lubricate your lock once or twice a year, or whenever it's hard to open or close. Insert the nozzle of a thin lubricant at the point where the bolt enters into the lock mechanism and insert

Fig. 17.7. Replacing pump grommet.

just a tiny squirt of oil. Also put some oil on the key, insert it in the lock, and then close and open the lock 2 or 3 times.

Pump

Once or twice a year, or whenever the pump works poorly, tighten the screw cap at the head. If the pump doesn't work, take the head apart. Sometimes you can get by with turning the flexible grommet around, or replace the grommet.

The rubber or plastic plunger inside the barrel can be reached by unscrewing the cap at the point where the plunger mechanism enters the barrel. Flex it, knead it, apply some lubricant to it, and if you can't get it to work replace the pump.

Appendix: Troubleshooting Guide

Problem or symptom	Possible cause	Solution	Chapter
High resistance while pedaling or coasting	1. Insufficient tire pressure 2. Rear wheel rubs on frame or accessory 3. Hub gearing need lubricating or adjusting	Inflate Adjust or straighten rear wheel Adjust, lubricate, or overhaul	4,6 3, 5 3,7
High resistance while pedaling, but not while coasting	1. Chain dirty, worn or not lubricated 2. Bottom bracket bearing needs adjusting 3. Pedal bearings need adjusting 4. Chain or chainring rubs on frame or accessory	Clean and lubricate, or replace Adjust and/or lubricate Adjust, lubricate, or replace Straighten or replace	8 3, 8 3, 8 8
Rubbing or scraping sounds	1. As above for high resistance when pedalling	See above	3, 8
Bike pulls to one side	1. Wheels misaligned 2. Front fork bent 3. Headset damaged 4. Frame misaligned	Adjust, center, align wheels Replace or straighten fork Overhaul or replace headset Get aligned or replace	7 14 3, 13 14
Bike vibrates at speed	1. Wheel rims bent ("out of true") 2. Headset loose 3. Hub bearings loose 4. Tire(s) installed unevenly	"True" wheel rims Adust headset Adjust hub bearings Deflate and reseat tire	7 3, 13 3, 7 6
Noises while pedaling	1. Chainring, cranks, or pedals loose 2. Chain dry, dirty, or worn 3. Bottom bracket or pedal bearings need adjusting	Fasten or replace Clean, lubricate, or replace Adjust and/or lubricate bearings	8 8 3, 8
Rubbing noises while pedaling	1. Gearing inside cog with outside chainring 2. Front derailleur misaligned	Select less extreme gear Adjust front derailleur mounting	9 9

Problem or symptom	Possible cause	Solution	Chapter
Chain drops off chainring or cog	1. Front or rear Derailleur range needs adjusting	Adjust derailleur range	9
	2. Chainring bent or loose	Straighten or tighten chainring	8
	3. Chainring and cog not aligned	Take to bike shop for correction	8
Chain jumps or skips off cog(s)	1. New chain on worn-out cog(s)	Replace smallest cog	9
	2. Bent chain links or tight link pin	Repair or replace chain	8, 9
Irregular pedaling motion	1. Crank, bottom bracket, or pedal bearing loose	Adjust bearings	3, 8
	2. Bent pedal spindle or crank	Replace pedal or crankset	8
Gears do not engage properly	1. Derailleur or derailleur range incorrectly adjusted	Adjust derailleur and range	9
	2. Damaged or dirty derailleur	Clean or replace derailleur	9
	3. Shift cable corroded or pinched	Clean, lubricate, adjust, or replace	3, 9
	4. Chain too short or too long	Replace chain or add/remove links	8
	5. Front derailleur loose or incorrectly mounted	Straighten and/or tighten derailleur	9
	6. Worn chain, chainring, or cogs	Replace	8, 9
Rim brake not effective	1. Rim or brake pads dirty, wet, or greasy	Clean, dry, and/or degrease	4, 11
	2. Brake pads worn	Replace brake pads	11
	3. Brake adjusted too loose	Readjust brake at lever or brake	11
	4. Brake cable pinched, corroded, or damaged	Replace brake cable	3, 11
	5. Brake lever loose or damaged	Replace brake lever	11
Rim brake rumbles	1. Brake caliper or brake arm(s) loose	Tighten brake or brake arms	11
	2. Wheel rim damaged, dirty, or greasy	Clean, true, or replace rim	4, 11
	3. Headset loose	Adjust headset	3, 13

Problem or symptom	Possible cause	Solution	Chapter
Rim brake squeals	1. As above for rim brake not effective 2. Brake pads not "toed in"	See above Adjust brake pads for "toe-in"	3, 4, 11 11
Disk brake not effective	1. Brake pads or disk dirty or pads worn 2. Hydraulic system has air trapped inside	Clean or adjust pads, clean disk Refer to bike shop for "bleeding"	12 12
Battery light defective	1. Batteries drained 2. Bulb defective 3. Contacts of battery, bulb, switch, or wiring defective 4. Switch defective	Replace and/or recharge batteries Replace bulb Clean, bend, or repair contact Replace switch or entire unit	17 17 17 17
Generator light defective	1. Bulb defective 2. Mass contact defective 3. Wiring defective 4. Generator slips off tire 5. Contact of generator, bulb, or wiring defective	Replace bulb Clean contact area, tighten screw Fix or replace wiring Bend installation hardware in Replace contact or unit	17 17 17 17 17
Uncomfortable riding position	1. Incorrect seat height or angle adjustment 2. Incorrect handlebar height or angle adjustment	Adjust seat Adjust handlebars	15 13
Accessory rattles or shifts	1. Attachment bolts not tight or bolts missing	Replace bolts and/or add protective plastic shim	4, 17
Suspension not responsive	1. Seals on stanchion (front) or shock (rear) dirty 2. Preload adjusted too high 3. Damage to stanchion (front) or shock unit (rear) 4. (Rear) pivots worn, corroded, or tight	Clean seals and surfaces Readjust preload setting Refer to bike shop Refer to bike shop	4, 16 16 16 16

Index